'This is a book I wish I had had at the start of my teaching career and one I will be happy to recommend to the many people I work with who support early careers teachers. I know both from personal experience and from extensive work in ITT and the early career phase that behaviour worries are amongst the biggest barriers to making progress as a new teacher. Behaviour is also one of the issues that has the biggest impact on wellbeing and emotional resilience. I particularly like the way the book uses a range of authors and perspectives to really dig into the underlying causes and helps build a fuller, more informed sense of the pupil as an individual with complex life circumstances impacting on how they show up.'

Samantha Twiselton, *Emeritus Professor and Former Founding Director of Sheffield Institute of Education (SIoE)*

'This is a refreshing book, encouraging teachers to reflect on behaviour with positive relationships, strength-based approaches and wellbeing at its heart. Providing a variety of perspectives shows that there is not one way of supporting pupils; voicing this is powerful! It allows readers to reflect on their own practice, while developing their understanding further, in a way that works for them, their pupils and their context. The key message for me was *"behaviour is not something to be managed but something to be made sense of to support"*, and this book provides us with the tools to do just that.'

Rachel Thynne, *SEMH Outreach Lead Teacher and author of* Behaviour Barriers and Beyond *and* Understanding Anxiety at School

Questions on Behaviour

What do I do when children don't seem to follow the rules? How can I create a classroom environment that promotes positive behaviour? How do I handle conflicts between students in a way that promotes inclusion?

Every teacher faces moments of uncertainty when managing behaviour in the classroom, and for Early Career Teachers (ECT) these challenges can feel especially daunting. Drawing on insights from a diverse panel of behaviour experts, this dip-in-and-out guide navigates these complexities with confidence, compassion, and curiosity, offering practical strategies rooted in real-life classroom experiences.

Each chapter provides actionable advice on topics ranging from classroom organisation and conflict resolution to handling individual and group behaviours. The guide goes beyond surface-level solutions, encouraging you to consider the 'why' behind behaviour while demystifying key concepts like 'warm/strict' approaches and trauma-informed practices. Contributors bring a wealth of expertise and lived experiences, and while perspectives may sometimes challenge your thinking, they collectively shape a classroom where every child feels safe, valued, and ready to learn. Case studies and reflections from the editor further invite you to deepen your understanding of the roots of behaviour and to strengthen your classroom practice.

Whether you're learning to establish routines, build connections, or navigate moments of disruption, *Questions on Behaviour* equips you with the tools to create a calm and inclusive learning environment. It will support you at every step of your teaching journey and is essential reading for ECTs, as well as a valuable staffroom resource for all educational settings.

Sarah Johnson is the founder and Director of Phoenix Education Consultancy, which works alongside educational establishments to identify their strengths and address gaps to improve outcomes for children and young people. With over twenty years of senior leadership experience across mainstream, alternative provision, and hospital education settings, she brings a depth of practical, relational understanding to questions of behaviour that few can match.

Sarah is President of PRUsAP, the national body for pupil referral units and alternative provision, and sits on Department for Education stakeholder groups for both AP and SEND. She is a member of the Special Education Consortium and a trustee of Bromley Y, a mental health charity supporting young people in South London. Her previous roles have included director of inclusion for a large primary school and head of a secondary pupil referral unit. She has also taught internationally, including in Uganda, which has deepened her commitment to culturally responsive, inclusive practice.

Q&As for ECTs Series

Questions on Teacher Wellbeing:
Creating a Happy and Sustainable School Life as an Early Career Teacher
Edited by Adrian Bethune and Emma Kell

Questions on SEND:
Developing Inclusive Practice as an Early Career Teacher
Edited by Georgina Durrant

Questions on Behaviour:
Building Classroom Confidence as an Early Career Teacher
Edited by Sarah Johnson

Questions on Safeguarding:
Developing Essential Safeguarding Skills as an Early Career Teacher
Edited by Sara Alston

Questions on Behaviour

Building Classroom Confidence as an Early Career Teacher

Edited by
Sarah Johnson

Routledge
Taylor & Francis Group
LONDON AND NEW YORK

Designed cover image: © Getty Images

First published 2027
by Routledge
4 Park Square, Milton Park, Abingdon, Oxon OX14 4RN

and by Routledge
605 Third Avenue, New York, NY 10158

Routledge is an imprint of the Taylor & Francis Group, an informa business

British Library Cataloguing-in-Publication Data
A catalogue record for this book is available from the British Library

ISBN: 9781032971551 (hbk)
ISBN: 9781032971506 (pbk)
ISBN: 9781003592426 (ebk)

DOI: 10.4324/9781003592426

Typeset in Optima
by Deanta Global Publishing Services, Chennai, India

Contents

Acronyms

ADHD	Attention Deficit Hyperactivity Disorder
AI	Artificial Intelligence
AP	Alternative Provision
CPD	Continual Professional Development
DfE	Department for Education
DSL	Designated Safeguarding Lead
ECEC	Early Childhood Education and Care
ECF	Early Career Framework
ECT	Early Career Teacher
EEF	Education Endowment Foundation
EHC	Education, Health, and Care
EHCP	Education, Health, and Care Plan
EYFS	Early Years Foundation Stage
KCSIE	Keeping Children Safe in Education
LA	Local Authority
MAT	Multi-Academy Trust
NASA	National Aeronautics and Space Administration
NQT	Newly Qualified Teacher
OBE	Order of the British Empire
PRU	Pupil Referral Unit
OFSTED	Office for Standards in Education
OSD	Offsite Directions
PSHE	Personal Social Health Education
SEMH	Social, Emotional, and Mental Health
SENCo	Special Educational Needs Coordinator
SEND	Special Educational Needs and Disabilities
SENDCo	Special Educational Needs and Disabilities Coordinator
SLT	Senior Leadership Team
TAs	Teaching Assistants
UK	United Kingdom

About the editor

Sarah Johnson is an educator, writer, and inclusion specialist whose career spans over 20 years in mainstream schools, PRUs, alternative provision (AP), and psychiatric in-patient education. She has worked at senior levels in local authorities overseeing behaviour and inclusion, and she is a member of the Department for Education's Alternative Provision stakeholder group, contributing to national policy, including the SEND and AP green paper. As Director of Phoenix Education Consultancy, Sarah support schools, trusts, and councils to embed evidence-informed, relational practice and to create fair, high-quality pathways for pupils with complex needs. She have advised the Youth Endowment Fund and the Ministry of Justice, chaired sector panels, and authored *Behaving Together: A Teacher's Guide to Nurturing Behaviour* and *All About SEMH*.

Beyond her professional role, she likes collecting random things, whether its feathers found on walks, objects with hidden stories, or fossils. Her house is made into a home by her children, her husband, and her cats.

About the contributors

Dr Sue Allingham started as a teacher, finally becoming a senior Early Years lead in a primary school and lead teacher for her local authority. Moving into research, Sue gained an MA and then a doctorate, both in Early Childhood Education, from the University of Sheffield. This led to becoming a local authority Early Years adviser, enabling her to develop her practice working with provision across the EYFS. As an independent consultant, author, and trainer, Sue is known for her practical style of working through coaching, mentoring, modelling, training, and working alongside teams to develop practice and provision. Her interests in teaching and learning have led to work on emotional and physical environments that will support informed teaching and learning through an understanding of neuroscience and physical development.

Sara Alston is a practising SENCo and safeguarding expert, with more than 38 years in classrooms and leadership roles. Now an independent consultant and trainer, she helps schools enhance SEND provision and safeguarding practices, writes regularly for educational publications, and has co-authored *The Inclusive Classroom* and *Working Effectively with Your TA*.

Phil Beadle is an award-winning teacher, author, and broadcaster known for his work on literacy, behaviour, and creative teaching. He has taught in some of the UK's most challenging schools and has written extensively on education, including *How to Teach* and *The Book of Plenary*. Phil is recognised for his engaging approach to classroom practice and his commitment to educational equity.

Mervin Cato brings 20 years of experience as an educationalist, serving schools and working in local authority settings in north London. He is committed to supporting families and communities, and has published *Your Family Needs You*, a practical guide based on his lived experience as an educator and family member to foster flourishing family dynamics.

Richard Clutterbuck brings nearly three decades of classroom and senior leadership experience to his current role as Head of Strategic Relations at Bromcom, a leading provider of management information systems for schools and multi-academy trusts (MATs). From 2011 to 2015, he served as Headteacher at Bristol Free School, then as Senior Principal at Cabot Learning Federation between 2016 and 2019. More recently, he returned to school leadership as Headteacher at Cirencester Deer Park School until 2024, helping shape its culture and standards.

David Didau is a writer, consultant, and former teacher with over two decades' experience in the classroom. Known for his blog *The Learning Spy*, he has written extensively on curriculum design, assessment, literacy, and the application of cognitive science to teaching. His books, including *Making Kids Cleverer, What If Everything You Knew About Education Was Wrong?*, and *Intelligent Accountability*, challenge received wisdom and provoke debate among teachers and school leaders. David works internationally with schools and education organisations, helping them improve teaching, learning, and leadership. His style combines scepticism with wit and a relentless commitment to evidence-informed practice.

Emma Dodds is Head of Student Services at Windsor Academy Trust. She has nearly two decades of experience in secondary education and has held a range of senior leadership positions. She has always held pastoral roles leading on safeguarding, attendance, inclusion, and behaviour. Emma has recently presented at the Department for Education's national conference.

Georgina Durrant is a former teacher, SENCo, and director of education, and the author of *100 Ways Your Child Can Learn Through Play*. She is the founder of *The SEN Resources Blog*, which supports parents and educators with practical advice, and regularly writes and speaks about inclusive practice and SEND.

Hannah Hall is an experienced educator and inclusion specialist with a background in teaching, SEND leadership, and whole-school development. She has worked across mainstream and alternative provision, supporting schools to build nurturing, high-expectation environments for all learners. Hannah is committed to evidence-informed practice and champions approaches that prioritise relationships, wellbeing, and inclusive curriculum design.

James Handscombe, OBE was educated at Silverdale School in Sheffield, after which he earned a first in mathematics at Oxford University and a master's from Harvard. Since qualifying as a teacher, he has worked in schools in South Wales, Australia, and London. In 2014, he was appointed Founding Principal of Harris Westminster Sixth Form and since 2022 has been Executive Principal of both Harris Westminster and Harris Clapham Sixth Form. His book *A School Built on Ethos* told the story of setting up Harris Westminster and explained how its success was built on the shared idea that learning is amazing. In his most recent book, *Cabinet of Curiosity*, he unpicks the power of inquisitiveness. He is known for his thought leadership in school ethos, often writing in *TES*, *Schools Week*, and *The Spectator*, and speaking at education events.

Clive Hill is an assistant principal for behaviour and attitudes, designing and running whole-school behaviour, safeguarding, and culture systems in complex secondary schools. A former non-commissioned officer in the British Army with an operational logistics background, he focuses on what actually works at scale. Clive has implemented phone-free models, rebuilt behaviour processes, and redesigned careers provision as a behavioural lever, using future pathways to re-engage students, raise expectations, and reduce persistent disruption.

Dr Haili Hughes is an experienced secondary school English teacher, former head of department, and senior leader, now serving as Director of Education at IRIS Connect and Principal Lecturer in Mentoring at the University of Sunderland. She has contributed to national policy as an ITT Quality Advisor for the Department for Education and is a member of the Teaching Commission. Drawing on her classroom expertise, she writes extensively on teacher retention, mentoring, and equity in education, and is the author of books including *Teaching to the Top* and *Beyond the Labels*.

Zoe Johal serves as Deputy Head and Designated Safeguarding Lead at Coventry Academy, a specialist provision. With a critical role in promoting the safety and welfare of students in an alternative provision context, she shapes both safeguarding culture and day-to-day pastoral support for vulnerable pupils.

Jenene Morgan is deputy headteacher at a secondary school in the London Brough of Redbridge, with a leadership focus on behaviour, culture, and inclusion. She plays a central role in shaping the school's approach to behaviour, ensuring that systems are consistent, fair, and rooted in positive relationships. Jenene's work emphasises that behaviour is not just about rules but about creating the conditions in which students feel safe, respected, and ready to learn. She supports staff in developing strategies that combine high expectations with empathy, equipping them to manage challenges while nurturing a strong sense of belonging across the school community.

Matt Morris has nearly two decades of experience across mainstream and alternative provision settings, originally training as an English teacher. Before joining TEAM Education Trust as Director of Transformation, he led an Alternative Provision academy, helping hundreds of vulnerable pupils who had previously been permanently excluded to develop social skills and transition to positive destinations. He now applies that insight across the trust, shaping teaching, leadership, and inclusion strategies.

Dr Daniel Owen is an experienced educationalist, having held a wide range of positions including subject leadership, school senior leadership, and a directorship in a multi-academy trust. Dan has experience as a school governor, member of a trust, and advisor on national and international pupil behaviour programmes and research projects. Dan has designed and led large-scale international school leadership development projects, written, taught, and assessed MA courses, supervised a number of MA theses, and been a doctoral supervisor.

Krupa Patel is a self-employed education consultant and coach with extensive experience working alongside schools and local authorities. She supports teaching and leadership development, especially through National Professional Qualifications (NPQs) and inclusive learning initiatives, bringing practical, in-school expertise to her consultancy work.

Philip Salisbury is a dedicated primary school headteacher working in a challenging Wolverhampton setting. Passionate about making a positive difference for children from deprived backgrounds, he leads with a focus on inspiration, wellbeing, and community engagement, such as organising memorable events like visits from Olympians to uplift pupils' aspirations.

Sarah Stevens is Executive Principal of Chiltern Academy Trust. She leads on inclusion and SEND across the school, focusing on creating supportive, high-expectation environments for all learners. Sarah has extensive experience developing whole-school approaches to behaviour and SEMH support, ensuring that inclusion is at the heart of school culture.

Enzo Vullo is an experienced teacher, author, and speaker with a particular focus on behaviour, inclusion, and literacy. He has taught in a range of schools and is known for his practical, relational approach to supporting pupils who struggle within traditional systems. Enzo writes and speaks widely about behaviour as communication, staff wellbeing, and creating classroom cultures where both students and teachers can succeed.

Steve Waters brings over 30 years of experience as a secondary school English teacher, department head, and assistant headteacher. He has channelled this into founding the Teach Well Alliance, promoting cultures of staff wellbeing in schools via the Teach Well Toolkit and his book *Cultures of Staff Wellbeing and Mental Health in Schools*. His practice-based approach centres on ensuring policy and leadership decisions prioritise teacher mental health and retention.

Cassie Young is Inclusion Executive Officer at Our Community Multi Academy Trust and an experienced primary headteacher. Formerly Head of School and SENCo at Brenzett CE Primary, she led the rapid turnaround of a school from "inadequate" by building an inclusive culture, strengthening community trust, and embedding high expectations for all learners. She now supports schools across the trust to develop equitable teaching and learning approaches.

Acknowledgements

Writing a book is often seen as a solitary act, but it is not. I have been overwhelmed by the generosity of the contributors who gave me not just their knowledge and expertise but their time. I thank them unreservedly for doing this and would be remiss not to. You can find out more about the contributors' viewpoints as the book unfolds.

I want to also say a thank you to Dan, my husband, who holds everything together when I am trying to juggle more than I probably should. When the balls do drop, as they so often do, you are the one quietly picking them up without fuss or fanfare. Thank you for making space for this work, and for me.

Thank you to my mum, one of my biggest supporters for as long as I can remember, and someone who has always, always believed in me. That belief has been the quiet foundation beneath everything. You are also one of the first to buy my books and to review them!

To Octavia, my eldest, who continues to teach me far more than I could ever teach her. Watching you grow has shaped how I think, how I write, and how I show up in this work.

And finally, to my younger daughters, Astrid, Iris, and Zelda: you remind me every day that behaviour needs to be supported at the earliest moments, and that co-regulation is not a theory but something lived in the small, ordinary exchanges of family life. All my children have shown me, in the most grounded way possible, what unconditional love actually looks like.

1

I'm here to teach, not deal with behaviour

It is a sentence that you have may have said yourself or heard in the school staffroom. It can be said in frustration after a difficult lesson, a disrupted activity, or a conversation that didn't go to plan. You may have said it because that is just how you feel. There is no shame in saying this: working with children, parents, and wider school organisations is hard work. If behaviour feels as though it is another barrier to you doing what you came to do – teach – then uttering this is completely understandable. I suspect that you decided to become a teacher to inspire children, to share your knowledge, and to help children grow into rounded adults. Despite these high aspirations, some days it feels as if the behaviour can get in the way of all of that.

If you've ever thought this, felt this, or said it out loud, you are not alone.

I still remember my own early days teaching PSHE (Personal Social Health Education) and Citizenship in an Inner London secondary school. Every Friday morning, Year 9 were chaotic. It didn't matter how carefully I planned my lesson. I would scour every resource, design interesting and engaging group activities, mix up the seating plan, think about the pace, pitch, and plenaries. It didn't matter.

DOI: 10.4324/9781003592426-1

Even before the door closed, the same thing happened. The students talked over me. Shouted out. Refused instructions. It was chaos,[1] and I dreaded it. Among all of this, I remember a child who sat at the back of the classroom. She was on the right-hand side, just by the exit. She was silent, too scared to talk, but she would always come to see me at lunchtime for a quiet break away from the hustle and bustle of the class. She was wonderful – all the children were wonderful – but I was ill-equipped and poorly supported to really make a dent in the behaviour, let alone be able to teach the subject in the way that I had planned and imagined. I clearly wasn't the only one who suffered from the feeling of chaos, and when I look back, I do feel that perhaps I should have done more to support her. I am glad she came and saw me at lunchtime, though, as it meant her quieter voice could still be heard.

My feelings around my own wellbeing reaffirm why the questions kick off in Chapter 2 with 'Starting from you'. This is a really important place. Without you, you can't change anything happening in or around the classroom.

Looking back at the behaviour of the Year 9 class, the difficulty arose only from a handful of students, but it dominated the room. It was pervasive, and the culture of that space was being taken over by distractions, lack of routine, and very little senior leadership support. The classroom behaviour left me feeling powerless and doubting myself. I was told my lessons weren't 'interesting enough', which only made the shame of what was occurring in the classroom even worse. I wanted to teach. I didn't want to spend every week managing shouting, avoidance, or disruption; I wanted to have the time and capacity to talk to that little girl sitting quietly at the back of the classroom. I didn't quite understand that this *was* still an integral part of teaching.

1 I initially wrote 'felt like chaos', but I don't want to start this book by lying to you. It was utter chaos.

Why do I feel like this?

This mindset 'I shouldn't have to deal with behaviour' is not just a personal response. It is shaped by how teacher training is structured, how schools are run, and how society views the role of teachers. When you are new, you are often the least experienced voice in the room. You may feel judged, even blamed, when a lesson does not go to plan. You may hear vague advice ('be more engaging', 'hold your ground') without anyone showing you how to do that. Or perhaps you've been given advice such as 'do not smile until Christmas'.[2] The strategies you *do* try may not seem to work straight away. All of that can leave you feeling isolated and overwhelmed.

It is no wonder, then, that managing behaviour ranks among the top reasons teachers leave the profession in the first five years. According to the Education Support Partnership (2023), stress related to behaviour and emotional needs in the classroom is one of the leading causes of attrition. Teacher Tapp (n.d.) data confirms it: behaviour is consistently the number-one thing teachers say they felt unprepared for when they started.

Yet despite these significant pressures, behaviour is often treated as an afterthought in training, policy, and public debate. When it is discussed, it is in simplistic and narrow debates that don't reveal much of the complexity of why children behave in the way they do and what we can do about it, Currently, discussions on curriculum and assessment reform dominate the agenda. But ask any teacher what is really making them consider leaving, and chances are it is not the phonics check or the curriculum; it is the daily, emotional pressures of trying to teach a lesson without the tools or support to do it confidently.

2 Just to let you know, it's fine to smile before Christmas. I read somewhere that you use more muscles smiling than frowning, or maybe it was fewer – I can't remember. Regardless, don't worry about smiling. It's a human thing to do to smile at other humans, even if they happen to be child humans.

Teaching behaviour is also teaching

Behaviour isn't a distraction from teaching; it's the foundation of it. Today, I picked my first courgette. I was ridiculously proud because 'green fingers' is not a phrase anyone would use about me. Cutting that courgette wasn't the beginning or the end; it was the result of a whole process: preparing the soil, watering, waiting for the sunshine, and battling my internal fury at slugs. Focusing on behaviour is the same – it's about creating the conditions that allow you to eventually reap the rewards of learning.

Every day, you're teaching more than just your subject. You're teaching children how to self-regulate, how to cope with frustration, how to speak respectfully, how to ask for help, and how to connect with others. Children don't come to school with these skills fully formed, and those who've faced trauma, exclusion, or unmet needs might have additional challenges which can form further barriers to learning.

Instead of asking:

> *Why do I have to deal with behaviour?*

Try asking:

> *What is this behaviour telling me about how this child is experiencing school?*

This doesn't mean you ignore disruption or never challenge behaviour. But it does means you begin from a place of curiosity rather than control. You have the power to notice patterns, to think more deeply about context, to try to work out what is happening. It doesn't mean it's your fault, but it does mean you might be able to influence change in what is happening in your class.

Do we need experts?

You might be thinking, 'But I don't know what I'm doing yet – I'm not the expert', and that might be the case, but you still have an inordinate amount to bring,

In 1998, NASA launched the Mars Climate Orbiter. It was a state-of-the-art spacecraft intended to study the Martian atmosphere. But due to a simple miscommunication between two engineering teams, one using metric units and the other using imperial, the spacecraft went wildly off course and disintegrated upon arrival – $125 million, gone in moments.

What went wrong? The investigation found three key failures: unchecked assumptions, lack of double checking, and overconfidence in routine systems. Teams assumed the experts had it right.

Sometimes experience can lead to automatic activity that doesn't encourage pause for reflection or thought. Fresh (and, hopefully, enthusiastic) eyes, like yours, have the potential to see things in different ways. This is why your questions matter, and this is why this book exists. Expertise is undoubtedly important, but so too is questioning, observing. Keeping our curiosity is what keep us learning.

Understanding behaviour across time

If you're thinking, 'Why is behaviour so bad now?', I invite you to take a broader view. Schools have always faced challenges when it comes to behaviour. When I was teaching a particularly challenging Year 9 class more than 20 years ago, this perspective brought me real comfort: It's not just me.

Behaviour difficulties are not a modern phenomenon; they've been part of school life for centuries. Take the Rugby School Rebellion of 1797[3] as an example.

3 One thing that is worth noting is that, according to *The Laurentian* (1898), there had been another riot, 11 years earlier, at the same school.

Dr Henry Ingles, Rugby's Headmaster at the time, was known for his strict disciplinary approach. The rebellion began when a student, Astley, was caught firing cork bullets at a housemaster's window. After being accused of lying about where he obtained the gunpowder, Astley was flogged. Outraged by this perceived injustice, his peers retaliated: they smashed windows, blew a door off its hinges, built a bonfire from school furniture, and barricaded themselves on a moated island on the school grounds.

> A petard was manufactured with the aid of an old gun-barrel, and with it the door of the sixth-form room was blown open.
>
> (The Laurentian, 1898)

The Headmaster responded by calling in the local authorities and, eventually, the army. The Riot Act was read aloud, formally ordering the students to disperse. When they did not, the army intervened. Several students were expelled, and corporal punishment resumed. This was not a minor disruption; it was a full-blown riot in one of England's most prestigious schools (Rugbeian Community, 2024).

When we think of behaviour in schools, we often imagine defiance, disruption, or disengagement. But sometimes behaviour becomes something bigger: a protest – a call for recognition, autonomy, and justice. In the spring of 1968, France witnessed a nationwide uprising that began with student protests and ended with ten million workers on strike. While the story of university students at Nanterre and the Sorbonne is well known, what is not so often told is the story of school-aged students, the lycéens.

Many of these young people were still in compulsory education, yet they formed their own action committees (comités d'action lycéens) and organised strikes, demonstrations, and occupations of school buildings. By mid-May, there were over 400 such committees operating across France (Wikipedia, 2024).

These students weren't simply reacting to unfair detentions or strict uniform rules. They were responding to a system that felt rigid, hierarchical, and disconnected from their lives. Their 'behaviour' – marching in the streets, building barricades, boycotting lessons – may have been misbehaviour, but it was *political*.

On 10 May 1968, during what would become known as the 'Night of the Barricades', hundreds of students, including school pupils, clashed with police in the Latin Quarter of Paris. The state responded with tear gas and batons, and the students with paving stones and makeshift shields. It was a full expression of the power struggle that can exist within educational systems when voice is denied and control outweighs dialogue (NPR, 2018; International Socialist Review, n.d.).

These events invite us to reconsider how we interpret behaviour in school settings. Behaviour is rarely just about the moment. It is shaped by power dynamics, histories, social identity, and the need for agency.

When students act out, shut down, or push back, what if, like the lycéens, they are trying to say something far more significant than we've been trained to hear?

Now, it's unlikely that your toughest day on duty has required reading the Riot Act or calling in the army or dealing with wider political instability (and I sincerely hope it never does). But these stories illustrate something vital. Behaviour is rarely just about behaviour. It reflects deeper dynamics, of power, justice (and injustice), belonging, and autonomy. The real question isn't 'Why is behaviour hard?' but how do we prevent it, how do we respond to it, and how can we learn from it?

What you can do now

You don't need to have it all figured out, and it's okay to feel nervous about how you might support children's behaviour. Here are some things that you *can* do:

- **Observe:** Watch how experienced staff start lessons. How do they greet students? When do they intervene?
- **Reflect:** When are things going well? What helps? What triggers things to go wrong?
- **Ask:** Find someone you trust and talk honestly about the moments that felt hard.
- **Start small:** Establish routines. Use calm, consistent responses. Hold your boundaries with kindness.
- **Build connection:** Learn students' names. Notice small wins. Celebrate effort.

You didn't train to teach to deal with shouting, swearing, or silence. You trained to teach. But to teach, you need trust. You need calm and you need community. Positive behaviour is one of the main ingredients to get there.

You might not feel like an expert now, but you *are* a teacher. And that means every moment you spend understanding behaviour is a moment spent shaping the learning of others.

How to use this book, for ECTs and beyond

The aim of this book is to build the confidence of Early Career Teachers (ECTs), but as I began to read the responses from the contributors, I realised I was learning so much too. Whether you're just starting out in the classroom or bringing with you a wealth of experience, this book has so much you can benefit from. For ECTs, it offers something beyond just a toolkit. It is a grounding in the real-world complexities of behaviour that you are likely to see in the classroom and wider school community. This book goes beyond surface-level strategies and instead explores the deeper roots that may mean you witness and experience disruption, disconnection, and defiance in the classroom. It helps you to move from simply reacting to reflecting on how you can craft your art as a teacher to support all children in your classroom. It is full of practical approaches, rich experiences shown in real-life classroom stories, and gentle prompts for self-reflection that aim to build confidence, foster relational practice, and help you develop a strong and calm presence.

For those more experienced classroom practitioners, this book becomes an opportunity to pause and to take stock. It invites you to reconnect with the 'why' behind behaviour, to consider patterns and not problems. It encourages you to notice the small moments that matter, and to bring a renewed sense of curiosity, compassion, and systemic awareness into your classroom.

This book goes beyond teachers; the huge accumulative experiences of executive head teachers, head teachers, teachers, and pastoral leaders means that this can be a powerful CPD (continual professional development) resource within your school community.

The structure of this book lends itself to help shape rich staff discussions, peer-led enquiry, and whole-school reflection. It can help shape learning walks, professional learning communities, or simply a conversation over tea about what really works.

This book is not a manual for those who want control or compliance, but one which reflects carefully on the professional relationship between teacher and students. It is a way of demonstrating how behaviour is not something to be *managed* but something to be made sense of and to support. Throughout this book, you'll encounter different, and sometimes conflicting, ways of understanding behaviour. That is intentional. Behaviour is complex, and so is the work of teaching.

Do all contributors agree with one another?

As you begin your journey in education, it's worth saying this clearly: feeling unsure, making mistakes, and questioning yourself are not signs that you are getting it wrong – they are signs that you are learning. Throughout your career, you will encounter a wide range of perspectives and viewpoints. Some will feel reassuring; others may feel challenging or even contradictory. That uncertainty is part of the work.

I find it helpful to think of these differences as *provocations* – not answers you must adopt, but invitations to pause, reflect, and think more deeply about the kind of teacher you are becoming. No one in education has everything figured out, even though it can sometimes appear that way. Our thinking evolves through experience and reflection, and, often, through things not going as planned.

The contributors to this book have shared their thinking from their own professional standpoints. They were chosen not because they all agree, but because they bring different lenses, questions, and challenges to the conversation. Together, they reflect the reality of education: complex, relational, and shaped by context.

As you move into Chapter 2, I invite you to read with curiosity rather than certainty. Take what resonates, sit with what feels uncomfortable, and allow yourself the freedom to change your mind over time. This book is not about having the 'right' answers; it is about supporting you to think, reflect, and grow with confidence, compassion, and a strong sense of purpose as you begin your career.

References

Education Support Partnership. (2023) *Teacher Wellbeing Index 2023*. London: Education Support. Available at: www.educationsupport.org.uk/media/0h4jd5pt/twix_2023.pdf

International Socialist Review. (n.d.) 'May 1968 and the revolt of the lycéens.' Available at: https://isreview.org/issue/111/may-1968-and-revolt-lyceens/index.html

The Laurentian. (1898) 'The Great Rebellion of 1797', The Rugby Racket. Available at: https://rugbyschool-mercury.cortes.websds.net/article/the-great-rebellion-of-1797?ref=

NPR. (2018) 'In France, The Protests Of May 1968 Reverberate Today – And Still Divide The French.' Available at: www.npr.org/sections/parallels/2018/05/29/613671633

Organisation for Economic Co-operation and Development (OECD). (2020) *Teachers and School Leaders as Valued Professionals: TALIS 2018 Results (Volume II)*. Paris: OECD Publishing. Available at: https://doi.org/10.1787/19cf08df-en

Rugbeian Community. (2024) 'Reading the Riot Act: Rugby School's "Great Rebellion" in 1797', Rugbeian Community. Available at: https://rugbeiancommunity.com/news/archive-news/325/325-Reading-the-Riot-Act-Rugby-Schools-Great-Rebellion-in-

Teacher Tapp. (n.d.) Insights and Trends from UK Classrooms. Available at: https://teachertapp.co.uk

Wikipedia. (2024) 'Comité d'action lycéen.' Available at: https://fr.wikipedia.org/wiki/Comit%C3%A9_d%27action_lyc%C3%A9en

2

Starting from you

Mental health, resilience, and the work of 'showing up'

Before you can manage a classroom, you must first learn to care for the person who walks into it each day, and that's *you*. The clichéd phrase 'You can't fill from an empty cup' is a clichéd one because it's one that is full of truth.

When we talk about behaviour in schools, we often focus on children, and rightly so. We talk about *their* emotions, *their* needs, and *their* choices. However, there is another key person in that room, and another story running alongside: the story of the adult in the room. You are the one that is trying to be steady, be present, and be kind in the face of mounting pressure.

This chapter begins with something personal. Many years ago, I read an article by the social worker and campaigner Peter Beresford titled 'We know madness and distress may be within us' (2002). I stuck it on the wall of where I worked and saw the title daily. I can't remember all of the article's content now, but the title has stayed with

DOI: 10.4324/9781003592426-2

me ever since. It cut through the silence around mental health and reminded me of something essential: none of us is immune to struggle. Stress, exhaustion, sadness, anxiety – these things are not signs of failure. They are part of being human. And they are particularly present when you are trying to become a teacher.

If you are reading this and wondering whether you're cut out for it – you might have had moments where you've sat on the edge of your bed in the morning and wondered how you'll get through the day – please know that you are not alone. You are not failing. For ECTs, this can be uncomfortable: schools can enable good behaviour practice, but they can also constrain it. Understanding systems does not mean agreeing with them; it means learning how to work ethically and effectively within them.

This chapter is a quiet but urgent invitation, to start with *you*. Not because self-care is a trendy buzzword, but because sustainability in this profession requires inner steadiness. You are your own most important tool in the classroom: your energy, your outlook, your ability to bounce back. You are not a tool that can be bought with more pay; your internal resources are more likely to keep you in the classroom than an increasing rage.

In the sections that follow, you'll hear from **Steve Waters**, founder of the Teach Well Toolkit and someone who understands deeply what it means to support the mental health of educators. He does not offer surface-level advice. Instead, he offers insight, honesty, and practical strategies for building resilience without guilt or perfectionism.

David Didau examines the emotional load of teaching, focusing on how ECTs can care for their own wellbeing in a demanding profession. Steve Waters shares strategies on managing workload, establishing boundaries, and advocating for yourself in school environments, while David Didau offers practical guidance on planning, marking, and balancing responsibilities when behaviour challenges mount. Together, they underscore that managing behaviour starts with sustaining the adult in the room.

We also explore how to stay emotionally present in the classroom, particularly in the face of challenging behaviour. You'll learn how to hold boundaries with compassion, how to stay grounded in tense moments, and how to recover afterwards. With this in mind, **Sarah Stevens** reminds us of the importance of remembering why you went into teaching in the first place.

This chapter doesn't just showcase when things go wrong, and it is certainly not about perfection, but it offers opportunities to reflect and improve.

If you ever feel that you are struggling, whether with behaviour, training, safeguarding, or any other aspect of your role, please remember: distress and exhaustion can affect us all. You are not weak. You are not failing. But you may need support. At the end of this chapter, I will signpost some useful resources. And I want to leave you with something I recently told a friend who was in crisis: 'I'll hold on to the hope, while you can't.'

Q How can I manage my workload effectively to prevent burnout?

> Burnout results when the balance of deadlines, demands, working hours, and other stressors outstrips rewards, recognition, and relaxation.
>
> (Michel, 2016)

A Managing your workload effectively as an Early Career Teacher (ECT) is crucial to preventing burnout. You will find yourself juggling lesson planning, classroom management, marking, and professional development. You may feel overwhelmed. However, there are several strategies that can help you manage your workload in a way that reduces stress and supports your long-term wellbeing.

1. Prioritise and organise your time

Start by mapping out your week. Use a digital calendar or planner to break down your tasks outside the classroom and the time you will spend on them. Prioritise what is most urgent and/or important, and allocate specific time slots for each task. Schedule your lesson planning, marking, and other administrative tasks. Build in breaks and set cut-off points when you are working after the end of the school day.

Look ahead to times when you might be overburdened – 'pinch points' – and plan how you will manage them. Anticipating stress and planning for it helps to reduce its impact.

2. Learn to say no and set boundaries

You may feel pressure to prove yourself by saying yes to every task or additional responsibility that comes your way. It is natural to want to create a good impression. However, this can lead to burnout. Setting boundaries and learning to say no respectfully is crucial to protecting your mental health.

3. Use digital tools and technology wisely

Digital tools can be a game changer in reducing workload if used effectively. From lesson planning to grading, several tools can streamline tasks and reduce the time spent on administrative work. Tools such as Google Classroom, Microsoft Teams, and Excel software can help speed up processes and free up time. Artificial intelligence (AI) tools, such as Open AI's Chat GPT, can help in a range of ways and is worth getting to know.

4. Work smarter, not harder

Working smarter means finding efficient ways to complete your tasks. For example, when planning lessons, consider reusing or adapting materials that have already been created, or collaborating with colleagues to share resources.

Establish a marking strategy that's manageable, within the school's policy, perhaps focusing on key assignments or using peer marking to lighten the load. Prioritise feedback that is most useful for your students' development.

5. Seek help and collaborate

Where possible, delegate tasks. For instance, if you have teaching assistants (TAs) or support staff, establish a relationship and ask for their advice. Collaboration can help you manage your workload more effectively and build a stronger support network.

6. Take care of your mental and physical health

Your wellbeing out of school is linked to your ability to manage your workload in school. Taking care of your physical and mental health is a priority. Set aside time for activities that help you relax and recharge - whether that's exercise, spending time with family or friends, or engaging in hobbies. Regular physical activity, like walking or running, reduces stress and maintains energy levels. Taking breaks during the day is also essential. Stepping away for a short walk or having a coffee break will help you return to your tasks with a clearer mind and better focus.

7. Monitor and reflect on your workload regularly

Conduct a 'workload audit' by reflecting on your tasks and identifying areas where you can reduce unnecessary work. For example, if administrative tasks are taking up too much time, discuss how they can be streamlined with your mentor or school leadership.

8. Develop a sustainable work routine

Maintaining a sustainable routine is key to wellbeing. Set a cut-off time for work each day, and stick to it. Allow time for relaxation and personal activities. It is also important to avoid overloading yourself during weekends. Balancing work with rest is crucial.

9. Understand that perfection is not always necessary

Teachers are often perfectionists. Embrace the idea that it's okay to make mistakes or to produce work that is 'good enough'. Striving for perfection in every task can lead to pressure and unrealistic expectations. Teaching is a continuous learning process, not a destination of flawless performance.

Managing your workload effectively as an ECT is crucial to avoiding burnout. By prioritising tasks, setting boundaries, and seeking support from colleagues, you can reduce stress and create a sustainable work–life balance. Taking care of your wellbeing is beneficial not only for you but for your students and your long-term career success.

Steve Waters

Q How can I advocate for myself when my wellbeing is being compromised by school demands?

A Advocating for your wellbeing as an ECT can be challenging, particularly when school demands feel overwhelming. ECTs often find themselves at a distance from school leadership, which can make it hard to voice concerns or seek support. However, it is essential to recognise that your mental health is not just important for you; it directly impacts your effectiveness as a teacher and your students' learning experiences. The key is to advocate for yourself in a way that is respectful, professional, and solution-oriented. Make a list of what is within your control and begin to make changes. Here are some strategies to help you to manage this process.

1. Recognise the importance of wellbeing

As an ECT, you are likely to be focused on meeting standards and expectations, managing your workload, and proving yourself in the classroom. However, the 2024 annual Teacher Wellbeing Index from Education Support shows that teachers are at risk of burnout, which can ultimately affect student outcomes. Acknowledge your needs and set boundaries that prioritise your wellbeing.

2. Set wellbeing non-negotiables

One effective strategy is to define your 'wellbeing non-negotiables'. These are the basic self-care practices you wish to prioritise. Non-negotiables might include ensuring you get a minimum amount of sleep each night, setting time aside for exercise, and making sure you have lunch away from your desk.

3. Use the One-Page Meeting strategy

A helpful resource in advocating for your wellbeing is Teach Well Toolkit's 'One-Page Meeting'. This strategy is designed to help you structure meetings with leadership or mentors in a way that enables you to communicate your needs effectively. In the example below, Ashley's mentor is herself on long-term sick leave. Ashley sends the following email to the Deputy Head who oversees ECTs:

> Dear Ms Roberts,
>
> I would be grateful if we could meet to discuss my workload.
>
> As a starting point, I have set out my concerns and potential solutions in the attached document.
>
> Thank you
>
> Ashley Cooper
>
> **Work overload**
>
> ***Key points***
>
> - I am finding my workload outside the classroom unsustainable.
> - I am concerned that I am unable to complete tasks in time.
> - I am working longer hours than some experienced staff members: 70 hours on average each week.

How work overload is affecting me

- My workload is eating into the time I have for my personal life.
- I am anxious and stressed at school. This is affecting my teaching.
- I am not sleeping properly.

Proposed solutions

- Please help me to prioritise my workload tasks.
- Recommend self-help courses to help me manage anxiety and stress.
- I would welcome regular wellbeing reviews of my workload to help me to action plan.

The impact of the solution

- More time to spend with my partner.
- Reduction in my anxiety/stress and better sleep.
- More effective teaching and classroom management.

Ashley Cooper

[Date]

By using the One-Page Meeting strategy, you influence the meeting to be more focused, solution-oriented, and proactive. It also ensures that you avoid the impression that you are just complaining.

Key points:

- As the name suggests, keep the proposed agenda to one page.
- The One-Page Meeting format ensures that you are respectful, professional, and solution-oriented.
- Three bullet points per heading.
- Take two printed copies of the agenda with you to the meeting, one for you and one for the person you are meeting (in case they have forgotten their copy).

- The purpose of the wellbeing review is to identify issues, reflect on your physical and mental health, assess the success of actions you have taken, and adjust your action plan to make progress.

4. Leverage mentorship and peer support

In most circumstances, your mentor or colleagues can provide vital support. They might also be able to suggest how to structure the One-Page Meeting. Talking to fellow ECTs or more experienced teachers can help you realise that you're not alone in feeling overwhelmed. Peer support allows you to share coping strategies and find collective solutions if staff identify school-wide issues.

5. Create healthy time boundaries

Time management is a crucial area to address when advocating for your wellbeing. Teachers often feel pressured to work beyond school hours, but it is important to establish boundaries early on. You might choose to limit work after a certain hour or during weekends.

Advocating for your wellbeing as an ECT is important for your physical and mental wellbeing and sustaining your career. By using strategies like the One-Page Meeting, setting wellbeing non-negotiables, and seeking mentorship support, you can maintain a healthy balance between your professional demands and personal health.

Steve Waters

Q How can I handle difficult classroom situations while preserving my mental wellbeing?

A school's approach to mental health and behaviour should be part of a consistent whole-school approach to mental health and wellbeing. This should involve providing a structured school environment with clear expectations of behaviour, well-communicated

> social norms and routines, which are reinforced with highly consistent consequence systems. This should be paired with an individualised graduated response when the behavioural issues might be a result of educational, mental health, other needs or vulnerabilities.
>
> (DfE, November 2018, updated in February 2024)

According to a National Behaviour Survey of teachers in May 2023 (DfE, April 2024), '73% of school leaders and teachers reported that pupil misbehaviour had had a negative impact on their health and wellbeing...in the past week'. An earlier study by Glazzard and Rose (2019) confirmed a relationship between teacher wellbeing and mental health and pupil progress in primary schools. Pupil misbehaviour, then, affects teachers' mental health which, in turn, affects pupil progress. Effective classroom management is important for your own wellbeing, as well as for pupil learning.

1. Establish clear boundaries and expectations

Set clear boundaries and expectations, within the framework of school rules and consequences. Consistency and clarity are key. When students know what is expected of them and understand the consequences of crossing boundaries, it reduces opportunities for off-task or disruptive behaviour. Predictability increases your control. Your aim should be to avoid difficult situations occurring in the first place.

When you are meeting a class for the first time, state your expectations. If you have your own classroom, make sure your expectations are displayed, and remind the class of them regularly. When you deal with individual distraction or misbehaviour, state how your expectations have not been met, and how you want the pupil(s) to change their behaviour. Consistency helps pupils to feel secure, and applying your classroom rules reduces stress and frustration.

2. Use positive reinforcement

An effective strategy is to use verbal praise and school reward systems to encourage positive behaviour. Recognising the class or individual students for even small achievements or good behaviour fosters a constructive classroom culture.

3. Develop strong teacher–student relationships

Building relationships with students is fundamental to managing difficult behaviour. When students feel that their teacher cares about them, they are more likely to engage and less likely to act out. As an ECT, you may feel that you don't have the experience to build such relationships, but even small gestures can make a big difference. Take time to get to know your students as individuals. Show interest in them, celebrate their successes, and express empathy when they face difficulties. A student who feels understood and valued is less likely to be disruptive, and when you do need to apply sanctions, you will have the rapport to move on from the incident.

4. Manage your stress with mindfulness breathing techniques

Teachers feel the weight of their classroom responsibility and the pressure to manage multiple tasks. As an ECT, the pressure can be more intense. When faced with challenging behaviour, stress can quickly escalate. One way to keep yourself calm in the classroom is to incorporate mindfulness and breathing techniques into your daily routine. Simple deep-breathing exercises, or taking a moment to pause and refocus, can help lower stress levels. For example, before addressing a disruptive student, take a few slow, deep breaths to regain composure. In moments of high tension, these pauses can enable you to respond thoughtfully rather than reacting impulsively.

5. Seek support from colleagues and mentors

As an ECT, you are not expected to have all the answers. Seek advice and support from more experienced colleagues and mentors. They have been where you are now. Mentoring support can provide a safe space to discuss your challenges. If a situation becomes particularly difficult, reach out to senior staff or the school's wellbeing lead for advice or assistance.

6. A calm-down area for pupils

Sometimes, pupils need a space to regulate their emotions before they can re-engage with the classroom. Having a designated 'calm-down' area – even if it is a single desk – in your classroom allows students to step away from difficult situations and regain control of their emotions. Or there might be a designated area in the school. Set clear guidelines for when and how students can use the calm-down space.

By setting clear expectations, reinforcing positive behaviour, seeking support, and practising avoiding reacting on impulse, you can prevent or effectively manage difficult classroom situations while preserving your mental wellbeing.

Steve Waters

Q What can do I do when I'm struggling to balance lesson planning, marking, and managing behaviour?

A Some weeks in teaching feel like a relentless balancing act, teetering between a thousand competing demands. There are lessons to prepare, pupils to respond to, expectations to meet. You start the morning with good intentions – a clear plan, a mental checklist – and by mid-afternoon, everything's shifted. A child's outburst derails the lesson. A stack of exercise books glares accusingly from your desk. You spend your lunch pleading with the photocopier, following up missed detentions, or searching for a glue stick that actually works.

Each one demands your attention, yet time and energy are finite. You begin the day hopeful, perhaps even excited, and end it exhausted, wondering how others make it all look so effortless. The truth is, they don't. Behind every calm exterior is a teacher who's learned to work with the chaos, not against it.

Let's start by thinking about out how to strip out some of the demands on planning. There's a quiet tyranny in the idea that every lesson needs to be a masterpiece – creative, original, endlessly engaging – but that kind of pressure quickly becomes paralysing. One of the best bits of advice I was given in my first year was to adopt a '1 in 4' mindset: if one in every four lessons is a belter, something that really sticks, students will forgive the other three for being a bit ordinary. Instead of chasing constant brilliance, focus on clarity. What's the one thing you want them to understand today? Build around that. Reuse effective routines. Start with the same, predictable retrieval activity every time – what happened last lesson? – and build from there. What do you want students to remember? What will they think about during the lesson? Remember, 'memory is the residue of thought' (Willingham, 2009, p.54).

There's a misguided belief that kids need variety. They get enough of this by trooping from subject to subject, teacher to teacher. Predictability is your ally. Work out a rhythm that works for you. Mine is: retrieval, explanation, shared practice, independent work. This isn't boring; it's efficient. Familiarity frees up thinking, both yours and theirs.

Then there's marking. It can feel never-ending, a pile that regenerates the moment your back is turned. But here, too, there's a better way. Mark less, give more feedback. Approaches like live-marking during lessons, whole-class feedback, and coded responses save time and often do more to improve learning than long written comments ever could. In fact, there's an inverse relationship between the length of a teacher's comment and the likelihood students are to read it. Not every piece of work needs a red pen. What matters is that students understand how to improve, and that they act on it. Feedback is only useful if it leads to student either aiming higher or working harder.

And, of course, behaviour. It's the invisible weight on your shoulders, the thing that makes everything else harder when it's not going well. But the answer isn't to be stricter or louder. Again, it's to be predictable. Clear routines, calm corrections, consistent follow-through: these are your most powerful tools. Always aim for certainty, not severity. Narrating the positive, setting simple rules, and applying them fairly will always outdo a complex routine or a stern lecture. Students don't need perfect teachers; they need safe, consistent ones.

Still, even with better systems in place, the workload can feel overwhelming. That's when triage becomes essential. Not everything needs doing *now*. Some things can wait. Some things don't need doing at all. Be ruthless in deciding what matters most: will this task help students learn, help me teach, or help me stay well? If not, it can go. For instance, I use a maximum of three slides per lesson. If you're given a slide deck by your head of department, you'll find that the vast majority of stuff on there is notes for teachers. Showing this stuff to students wastes everybody's time.

Finally, and perhaps most importantly, don't do it alone. Teaching is not an individual pursuit. Borrow resources, ask questions, share problems. Someone in your department has likely faced and solved the same issues. Talk to them. Laugh with them. Let them tell you it's normal to feel like this. Because it is.

There's no magic fix for the balancing act. But you can steady your feet. Reduce the weight. Share the load. And slowly, you'll find that what once felt impossible starts to feel manageable – some days even joyful. Most importantly, know that it won't always be this hard. You're not failing. You're learning. And you're doing better than you think.

David Didau

Q How can I find joy in teaching and truly celebrate the positive impact I have on my students' lives, especially when the challenges of the classroom sometimes feel overwhelming?

A This is such an important question, and one that is important not to lose sight of when the going gets tough. I think every teacher, no matter how experienced, revisits this throughout their career. Teaching is a profession filled with so many moments of joy, but it's also one of the most demanding jobs there are. Between lesson planning, assessment, break duties and the emotional energy that students draw from us each day, it's easy to lose sight of the reasons that first drew us into education. Yet finding, and, perhaps most importantly, holding on to that, is essential for your wellbeing and for the lasting impact you'll have on your students.

Let's start with a truth worth remembering: you are already making a difference, even if you can't see it. Your influence extends far beyond the moments you witness in the classroom. Every time you greet a student by name, ask them about their hobbies, encourage them to keep trying, or take a moment to listen when they're struggling, you're valuing them and shaping their sense of self-worth. These are the moments that live on long after the lesson ends. Sometimes the impact is visible – a student mastering a concept, smiling with pride, or thanking you years later. But often it's quiet and unseen. Learning to trust in that unseen impact is part of the joy of teaching.

One way to nurture that trust is to celebrate the little things. In education, progress can be incremental and easily overlooked if we only focus on the big outcomes. Did a previously withdrawn student raise their hand today? Did your class respond thoughtfully to a question that once left them silent? Did you manage to adapt a lesson in a way that reached a student who usually struggles? These are moments worth noticing. Note some daily wins. Over time, that collection becomes a tangible reminder of how far you and your students have come together.

It's also vital to reconnect with your 'why'. Think back to what inspired you to become a teacher. Maybe it was a love of your subject, a teacher who once believed in you, or a desire to help others see their own potential. In the middle of hectic school life, that original spark can fade beneath the weight of deadlines and data. Take time to rekindle it. Revisit the parts of teaching that create a spark in you – perhaps it's creative lesson design, storytelling, mentoring, or seeing the world through your students' curiosity. Make time for these moments.

Another way to sustain joy is through connection with people – both with students and colleagues. Relationships are the beating heart of teaching. Make time to laugh with your students, share their excitement, and show them that you are human too. Genuine connection fosters trust, and trust creates a classroom atmosphere where learning can flourish. Equally, lean on your colleagues. Teaching can sometimes feel solitary, but you're part of a community that understands exactly what you're experiencing. Share stories, swap ideas, and celebrate each other's wins. A quick chat in the staffroom about a small success can be surprisingly uplifting. Be the positive influence in that space, encouraging longer-serving colleagues to reconnect with their joy.

Of course, joy in teaching also grows from an appropriate work–life balance. Early in your career, it's tempting to give everything to your students, but remember you can't pour from an empty cup. Setting boundaries, resting, and nurturing your life outside school are essential acts of sustainability. When you look after yourself, you bring more energy, patience, and creativity back into the classroom, which benefits your students. Eat well and get your vitamins! We all know that schools are hotbeds of bugs.

Finally, remember to reflect. Teaching moves very quickly, and we rarely get the chance to step back and appreciate what we've achieved. At the end of each term, take a minute to look at the progress your students have made both academically and personally. Who has grown in confidence? Who now believes they can succeed because of something you said or did? Reflection transforms experience into meaning, and meaning fuels joy.

So yes, there will undoubtedly be challenging days, the kind that leave you questioning whether you're making any difference at all. But there will also be far more days of laughter, insight, and connection that remind you why you chose this path. Teaching is a profoundly human profession: unpredictable, emotional, and endlessly rewarding. If you can find moments of joy amid the chaos, celebrate the small triumphs, and trust that your influence truly matters – because believe me it does – then you're already succeeding in the most important way.

Teacher life is a roller coaster, with big ups and downs. Celebrate the highs, reflect on the lows, and enjoy the ride!

Sarah Stevens

Further support: Wellbeing organisations for educators (UK)

You do not have to navigate this journey alone. Whether you need confidential advice, emotional support, or practical resources to protect your mental health, there are organisations dedicated to helping teachers and education staff. The following are some trusted UK-based services to explore:

1. Education Support

www.educationsupport.org.uk

A UK charity dedicated to the mental health and wellbeing of teachers and education staff. Offers free 24/7 helpline support, wellbeing webinars, grants, and resources.

Free helpline: 08000 562 561 (UK-wide)

2. Teach Well Alliance

www.teachwellalliance.com

Founded by Steve Waters, this organisation offers training, consultancy, and a structured framework (Teach Well Toolkit) to help schools develop a whole-school approach to mental health and wellbeing.

3. Mind (Education Staff)

www.mind.org.uk/workplace/mental-health-at-work/taking-care-of-your-staff

National mental health charity with specific guidance for school staff and employers. Offers toolkits for stress, anxiety, and mental health awareness in the workplace.

4. Anna Freud Centre – Mentally Healthy Schools

www.mentallyhealthyschools.org.uk

A rich resource hub for school staff including mental health teaching resources, signposting, and whole-school approaches to wellbeing.

5. The Chartered College of Teaching – Teacher Wellbeing

www.chartered.college

Publishes evidence-informed articles and resources for teachers, including research on wellbeing and workload. Membership gives access to journals and networks.

6. NHS Every Mind Matters

www.nhs.uk/every-mind-matters

Offers personalised mental health action plans, advice on anxiety, low mood, and stress, and links to professional services.

If you are struggling and feel overwhelmed, reach out. Speak to your mentor, your line manager, or your GP. You deserve support, not just because you are a teacher, but because you are a person.

Reflective questions

- How am I currently looking after my own wellbeing, and what small changes could I make to protect myself?
- Which workload management strategies discussed in this chapter feel most achievable for me right now, and how might I begin to implement one or two of them?
- When faced with challenging behaviour in the classroom, how do I typically respond, and how might I adjust my approach to support my wellbeing
- Who can I turn to for support when I feel overwhelmed?

References

Beresford, P. (2002) 'We know madness and distress may be within us', *The Independent*, 14 March. Available at: www.independent.co.uk/voices/commentators/peter-beresford-we-know-madness-and-distress-may-be-within-us-9204197.html

Department for Education (DfE). (November 2018) *Mental Health and Behaviour in Schools*. Available at: https://assets.publishing.service.gov.uk/media/625ee6148fa8f54a8bb65ba9/Mental_health_and_behaviour_in_schools.pdf

Department for Education (DfE). (February 2024) *Behaviour in Schools: Advice for headteachers and school staff.* Available at: https://assets.publishing.service.gov.uk/media/65ce3721e1bdec001a3221fe/Behaviour_in_schools_-_advice_for_headteachers_and_school_staff_Feb_2024.pdf

Department for Education (DfE). (April 2024) *National Behaviour Survey: Findings from Academic Year 2022/23*. Available at: https://assets.publishing.service.gov.uk/media/6836f84b8ade4d13a63236c0/National_behaviour_survey_AY_2022_2023_report.pdf

Education Support. (2024) *Teacher Wellbeing Index*. Available at: www.educationsupport.org.uk/media/ftwl04cs/twix-2024.pdf

Glazzard, J. and Rose, A. (2019) 'The impact of teacher well-being and mental health on pupil progress in primary schools.' Leeds Beckett University. Available at: https://eprints.leedsbeckett.ac.uk/id/eprint/6268/1

Michel, A. (2016) 'Burnout and the brain', *Observer*, 29, no. 2 (February). Washington, DC: Association for Psychological Science. Available at: www.psychologicalscience.org/observer/burnout-and-the-brain

Teach Well Toolkit. The One-Page Meeting. Download free at: www.teachwelltoolkit.com

Willingham, D. T. (2009) *Why Don't Students Like School?* San Francisco: Jossey-Bass.

3

Schools and trusts as organisations

When we talk about behaviour, it is tempting to focus on individual children, difficult lessons, or challenging weeks. These moments matter, but they rarely tell the whole story. Behaviour does not happen in isolation. Every classroom sits within a wider system, and the actions teachers take – consciously or not – contribute to the culture of the school and the organisation around it. This chapter invites you to step back and examine that bigger picture.

Early in your career, it can feel as though your influence ends at the classroom door. In reality, the opposite is true. Whether you are an Early Career Teacher (ECT) or an experienced leader, your everyday practices – how you greet students, enforce routines, speak about colleagues, or respond to families – help to shape and sustain school culture. Schools are not just collections of policies and procedures; they are complex, relational systems made up of people, power, trust, and shared values.

Understanding behaviour through this systems lens is essential, but it can also be uncomfortable. Systems enable good practice, but they can also constrain it. Teachers are asked to exercise professional judgement while working within frameworks they did not design and

 DOI: 10.4324/9781003592426-3

cannot control. This chapter does not pretend that tension doesn't exist. Instead, it helps you understand how schools, trusts, and local authorities influence behaviour practice – and how teachers can act with integrity within those structures.

To explore this complexity, the chapter brings together contributors who examine behaviour from multiple organisational perspectives. **James Handscombe, OBE** opens the chapter by drawing on organisational theory to show that schools are not rigid hierarchies but dynamic blends of power, role, task, and personal responsibility. His contribution helps ECTs understand the often-invisible structures of school life and how to navigate them professionally and ethically.

Dr Haili Hughes offers two companion pieces that bring the focus back to daily practice. First, she explores how school ethos is lived, not written – shaped through consistent, relational behaviour practice rather than posters or policies. In her second contribution, she turns to collaboration, highlighting how consistency in behaviour management depends on shared understanding between teachers, support staff, and leaders. Her work reminds ECTs that they are not passive recipients of culture; they are active participants in shaping it.

Moving beyond individual schools, **Matt Morris** and **Mervin Cato** examine the roles of multi-academy trusts and local authorities, showing how decisions made at system level shape behaviour policy, inclusion, and support in ways that are often invisible to classroom teachers. **Emma Dodds** brings a leadership perspective to high-stakes decision making around suspensions and exclusions, foregrounding the human stories behind these choices and their long-term impact on belonging and trust.

The chapter also draws learning from specialist contexts. **Zoe Johal** and **Matt Morris** explore practice in special schools and alternative provision, illustrating how consistency, empathy, and relationship-centred approaches can create safety and structure even in highly complex settings. These insights challenge assumptions about what is possible and offer transferable lessons for all schools.

Threaded throughout the chapter is the role of parents and carers. Behaviour is not experienced by families through policy documents, but through their children's stories, their trust in staff, and the everyday interactions that shape reputation and belief. Parents and carers are not bystanders in school culture; they are influential stakeholders whose perceptions and experiences shape how behaviour systems are understood and sustained.

Taken together, this chapter reaffirms that behaviour cannot be separated from culture, and culture cannot be separated from the wider system. As an ECT, you are not operating on the margins of that system but as an integral of it. By understanding the structures, relationships, and voices that are within and beyond your classroom; including those of families, you place yourself in a stronger position to act ethically, professionally, and with moral purpose.

Q How do schools actually work?

A In *Inside Organisations*, Charles Handy (1999) tells us that there are four possible command structures for an organisation – Power, Role, Task, and Person – and that making the organisation work for you requires you to understand which one you're in. The Power structure is a small business where your influence depends on how much the owner trusts you; the Role structure is the army where you answer to those above you and control those below; Task structure is a modern consultancy where teams are put together based on their skills; and Person structure is an artist's collective where everyone does their own thing and shares some common facilities. You, however, are in a school (unless you're in a bookshop and have picked this up because you liked the cover and are leafing through to while away a few minutes – in which case who knew we'd do so well?). Which of these structures do you need to understand to navigate your workplace?

Unfortunately, Handy's guide fails us a little here (and to be fair to him, he wrote an entirely different book in 1990 called *Understanding Schools as Organisations*). Schools contain a bit of each of these models, rubbing up against each other, overlapping, and conflicting, and, worse, each school has the four cultures in their own proportions. To get the support you need and the recognition you deserve, and to avoid getting caught up in politics or being frustrated by bureaucracy, you need to understand how the four fit together and to work out which structure is dominating your situation.

First, Power: the head of a school has a lot of responsibility and a lot of power – all the strands of discipline, budgeting, HR, and governance will come together on their desk. Some heads are more trusting than others, some delegate more, but ultimately it is their name on the board outside, their head on the block, and so to some extent everything depends on them.

My tips for navigating this are:

- Pick a school with a head you want to work for.
- Maintain your personal credit – be reliable, do your best work if they ask you to do something, don't presume on their goodwill.
- Don't let office politics take you away from what's important – remember this is only part of the story.

Role: teachers are employed to fill a gap in the timetable – when the advert went up for 'Teacher of Geography' (or whatever role you applied for), it was, fundamentally, because the school needed an adult in that classroom for those hours. The line-management structures of a school are typically very hierarchical: the head will line-manage deputies who line-manage middle leaders who line-manage everyone else. It's easy to feel as though you're in a military sausage machine. My tips are:

- Take comfort in the knowledge that, at a fundamental level, if you stop hell breaking loose in your classroom during your lessons, then you've done your job.

- Use the line-management structure. Take problems to your immediate boss, use the support they give you.
- Don't let yourself believe the sausage-factory model. Schools are relatively small organisations that are very people-centred: the organogram might look military, but the relationships are personal.

Task: this is the structure favoured by bright graduates – as one yourself, it is likely to be one that you're drawn to, where the best people for each job are chosen based on an objective evaluation of their skills. Unfortunately, it's the structure that is least suited to schoolwork – there are occasional working parties, but these tend to be alliances of the willing rather than chosen on merit. Some tips:

- Take part in working parties, teams, and groups when they come up – it's fun, you're likely to learn from the people there, and, hopefully, you'll get a lot done.
- Don't get frustrated that schools are like schools. Certainly, don't try to restructure them to fit your own preferences – that road leads to endless wailing and gnashing of teeth.

Person: the bottom line is that for most of the day you're alone in your classroom – alone, that is, except for the students in your care. You have a lot of responsibility, little supervision, and a huge amount of freedom to choose how things go (in theory, at least – the challenges of managing a couple of dozen students means there are always compromises and exceptions). A final set of tips:

- Make professional choices. You're in charge of your own classroom, and you have responsibility for the welfare and education of these young people – the most junior ECT in any school is an important leader.
- Use your freedoms. You will get lots of advice from lots of people (including the last page or so from me) – listen to it, think about it, try it out, but feel free to disregard it if it doesn't work for you.

- Don't go rogue. Your classroom is your space, but it fits within the wider school – what you do affects your colleagues. If you undermine them, then they will have less inclination to support you when you need it.

Schools are incredibly complex organisations, but they are truly wonderful ones doing incredible work. The way people work together varies hugely depending on the context – doing your job and being a good colleague means understanding the prevailing paradigm. Good luck!

James Handscombe, OBE

Q How can I promote the ethos of a school as an ECT?

A As an ECT, you play a pivotal role in promoting and sustaining the school's ethos, particularly concerning behaviour management. Establishing a positive behavioural culture is essential for creating an environment conducive to learning and personal development. This is often something ECTs really struggle with. I am lucky enough to work with thousands of new teachers every year, and, almost universally, they state that behaviour is one of their biggest worries and challenges. I always reply that it is all about culture and consistency.

Understanding and embodying the school's behavioural ethos

A school's ethos encompasses its core values, beliefs, and behavioural expectations. For ECTs, comprehending and internalising this ethos is the first step towards effective behaviour management. Research indicates that when teachers align their practices with the school's values, it fosters consistency and clarity for students, thereby enhancing behavioural outcomes (Starkey, 2023).

In my first school, the ethos was one of trust and mutual respect between students and staff – but this was not always easy to uphold! Teenagers can be challenging, and there were times when I definitely lost my cool, responding in a way that probably antagonised students rather than calmed down a situation. Of course, we are only human, but there are some practical ways to avoid falling into that trap.

It starts by engaging with the school's policies. Thoroughly review the school's behaviour policies, codes of conduct, and mission statements, and ensure that these are the consistent guiding star that underpins decision making and actions. There may be times when you don't agree with the school's stance, but this should never be communicated to pupils. If it is, there is a risk you let down and undermine other colleagues who are holding the line. If things get tricky, seek advice and support from your mentor or another experienced colleague. This might include observing and discussing effective behaviour management strategies that reflect the school's values. One of the most useful things I ever did as a new teacher was to observe a class I taught and was having difficulties with in another subject area, with a very experienced colleague. I was shocked to see how different their behaviour was with this teacher, and it was largely down to presence. But how can you replicate that? Through conversations with the colleague about their decision making, I was able to codify and adapt their strategies to help improve the climate in my own classroom. By immersing themselves in the school's behavioural framework, ECTs can model and reinforce the desired conduct among students.

Establishing consistent classroom routines is also key. Consistency in classroom routines is fundamental to promoting positive behaviour. The Education Endowment Foundation (EEF) emphasises that clear routines help students understand expectations, reducing behavioural issues (EEF, 2019). It starts with the setting of clear expectations. Teachers need to clearly articulate behavioural expectations at the outset and revisit them regularly. Establishing routines for common classroom activities, such as entering the room, transitioning between tasks, and seeking help, will also help students develop an automaticity for these tasks, freeing up cognitive load to be able to focus on what really matters: learning. Consistent reinforcement is also vital. Apply rules and consequences consistently to maintain fairness and predictability. By fostering a structured environment, ECTs can minimise disruptions and promote a culture of respect and responsibility.

Of course, a lot of this comes down to building positive relationships. Strong teacher–student relationships are integral to effective behaviour management. Positive interactions can lead to increased student engagement and reduced behavioural problems (Cramond, 2021). To cultivate these relationships, you should demonstrate empathy and respect. Showing genuine interest in students' wellbeing and perspectives helps students feel seen. This could be as simple as asking about a hobby or remembering something they told you. This builds that sense of belonging and psychological safety that is part of human-centred leadership.

It is also not just focusing on negative behaviours. Offering feedback that acknowledges positive behaviour and guides improvements encourages students to want to do the right thing.

Mostly, it is about being proactive. Proactive strategies focus on preventing behavioural issues before they arise. The Department for Education's *Creating a Culture* report highlights the importance of proactive approaches in establishing a positive behavioural culture (Department for Education, 2017). These include giving positive reinforcement, recognising and rewarding appropriate behaviour to encourage its recurrence. Early intervention is also vital; addressing minor misbehaviours promptly to prevent escalation fosters a classroom environment where positive behaviour is the norm, reflecting the school's ethos.

Dr Haili Hughes

Q What is the role of the wider trust in behaviour in my classroom?

A With regard to behaviour, the role of a multi-academy trust (MAT) is very much akin to that of a school. Trusts set the vision and philosophy for behaviour and play a role in ensuring schools are highly effective learning environments. The obvious key differences between schools and trusts is the scale at which policy and practice is delivered. Trusts may have additional resources which can support staff development and the implementation of a behavioural policy.

Philosophical approaches to behaviour differ from trust to trust: while some prefer relational approaches to traditional behaviour models, others culture a zero-tolerance attitude towards poor behaviour. Restorative practice is increasingly common, as are policies built upon trauma awareness.

The application of these philosophies differs from trust to trust also. It's common for trusts to expect all their schools to strictly follow the same policy and procedures, with high expectations regarding uniformity of practice. The rationale for this is that consistency allows for individuals to move between trust schools while maintaining the same expectations. Adversely, trusts might adopt an approach where they outline an overarching policy but the practice in each of the trust's schools is dictated by the context of the school and its pupils. For example, a special school and a mainstream primary in the same trust would have very different needs and may likely need staff to be trained differently.

Given that trusts can pool resources from across their schools, they are able to offer comprehensive programmes of continuing professional development, coaching, and personalised or targeted support. Given also the wealth of knowledge within a MAT, the trust CPD programmes centred on behaviour may offer an insight into a wide range of behaviour issues, theoretical approaches to the management of behaviour, and classroom management strategies, often providing a level of training that goes beyond the guidelines of the behaviour policy.

Trusts are also well positioned to provide specialist support and intervention. While the strong classroom management practices of teachers go a long way to create the desired environment for effective learning to take place, MATs have support structures that are more progressive than those provided by an individual school. MATs often have behaviour leads to model the expected practice of the organisation and who can offer targeted support and guidance. Trusts may also have inclusion teams or leads to work with pupils who have an elevated level of need and require a more bespoke approach. Behaviour and inclusion leads can support in the creation of personalised behaviour support plans and risk assessments for pupils and can help school staff to identify the triggers and strategies of an individual child.

Some trusts will also provide inclusive pathways or interventions for pupils who may be at risk of permanent exclusion. Those interventions may be a combination of alternative provision (AP), in-house interventions or units, or alternative curriculum pathways as part of the mainstream curriculum. Where schools commission alternative provision for pupils, it is the responsibility of the school to ensure that the AP is suitable and safe, and can provide high-quality education provision. Many trusts undertake this quality assurance on behalf of their schools using a standards framework of their own devising. Should a child be permanently excluded from school, national guidance requires the governing board to consider the reinstatement of the child. The same guidance allows for the trust board to take on this role instead of the local governing body, where a school is an academy. Where this is the case, it must be set out clearly within the trust's suspension and exclusion policy.

Sanction and reward are inherent to any behaviour policy; the best policies and practice extensively promote praise and reward. In trust behaviour policies this is no different; however, trusts may offer an additional tier of reward and recognition. For example, many trusts have rewards which complement the school's own rewards system and provide increased opportunity for young people to be recognised for their efforts and achievements.

As an ECT, it is essential that you strike a balance of developing your own strategies for behaviour and classroom management, while remaining consistent with the school or trust philosophy. Familiarity with the trust behaviour policy will help you to develop consistent practice and the ability to apply said practice with confidence. Knowing that the trust provides support for teachers and pupils can give new and developing teachers further confidence in the correct application of *the trust way*.

Matt Morris

Q What can we learn from special schools about behaviour?

A At some point during your journey to becoming a fully qualified teacher, you'll no doubt hear the phrase 'all behaviour is communication'. This is inaccurate for many reasons, most notably that there are a wide range of other factors, some short-term and some longstanding, that affect the behaviour of children. There's also the often inconvenient truth that some children choose to behave in a manner that we might not traditionally view as appropriate, for no discernible reason. That said, if we look at the teaching of children with communication challenges, we can adopt a different mindset when responding to challenging behaviour.

Where children are non-verbal, have limited language skills, autism, or social, emotional, and mental health (SEMH) needs, some of their behaviours are born out of frustration when trying to communicate. Episodic behaviour such as withdrawal and meltdowns can often be an indicator that a child is overwhelmed, suffering from anxiety, or struggling to express themselves. Teachers in special schools will therefore seek to understand the behaviour, separating this from the child, rather than attempting to control it. Consider asking yourself these questions: What has caused the child to behave in this way? What is the child trying to tell me?

In special schools, individual support plans and risk assessments are integral to supporting the needs and triggers associated with a given child. Knowledge of those triggers, aligned to the strategies known to work and what steps or language to avoid, allow special school teachers to plan positively and mitigate ahead of time. The response to behaviour is very much proactive, rather than reactive. While such plans are used in mainstream schools, they tend to be only in place for a small number of pupils with persistent behaviour challenges.

You may question whether approaches that require a level of planning for every child are possible in mainstream settings, where class sizes are likely to be much larger. Although this might feel like an insurmountable or onerous task, it's the principles or small steps that can make a difference. Think of it this way: *every interaction is an intervention*; while special school curricula are built upon interventions, the smallest interactions that you have with children can still have an enormous impact. Just remember, this works both positively and negatively.

In many specialist settings, the school staff are highly trained in de-escalation techniques and interventions which are non-restrictive. It is a common misconception that the programme of strategies taught to staff, which are often referred to as *positive behaviour support* or *positive handling*, are purely training in physical interventions. In reality, these programmes have clear principles, where 95 per cent of the application is de-escalation and communication, and the 5 per cent which is physical intervention is intended as a last resort. The strategies for de-escalation, such as offering space, time, and choices to pupils, help them to regulate and regain control, and often pre-empt further dysregulation. These strategies are equally as effective in mainstream settings, and can be vital tools in any teacher's approach.

Many special school pupils are taught how to regulate their emotions, and they work with teaching staff to develop individualised routines and strategies. In schools where staff are trained to model patience and composure, and to maintain a calm façade even in the face of adversity or stress, staff and pupils can *co-regulate*. Co-regulation is the idea that dysregulated children need regulated adults to more effectively reach a calm state. For a new teacher, being regulated means being mindful of your tone of voice, remaining calm, and stepping back from heightened situations, and only using non-threatening cues and body language. The most effective teachers are those who able to recognise and respond to their own emotional triggers and responses to distressing or pressurised circumstances.

Good behaviour is built upon clear and consistent routines and structures, which pupils understand and can even predict. Mainstream schools can draw upon some of the tools used in special schools which support pupils to understand the routines, underpin expectations, and create the mindset of a safe learning environment. Tools such as visual timetables, now and next boards, cue cards, and the use of different boards in the room for different tasks, or to distinguish between routine information and learning, are all valuable classroom management devices, regardless of the type of school or ability of the pupil.

Most strategies and techniques used in special schools can be equally effective in mainstream schools, and many of those strategies more frequently feature in the mainstream classroom. The important thing to remember is to find the right tools to meet the needs of your pupils, and to be unafraid of trialling different approaches in the pursuit of creating a positive classroom environment where pupils are able to flourish.

Matt Morris

Q Why do leaders make the decisions they do? Suspension and permanent exclusion

A 'Don't smile until Christmas.' This was once a common piece of advice offered to trainees during behaviour management training. The message was clear: don't let them see any weakness until you have them in check and have established control. The 'them' are children, children who are developing and getting to know themselves, navigating emotions, and finding their eventual place in the world. Can you imagine how it would feel as an adult in a new job if no one smiled at you for the first four months?

Leaders are often faced with incredibly challenging decisions, often all at once, so that sometimes it can feel like spinning plates; add a dysregulated child into this and an equally emotional charged adult who is after a pound of flesh because a child dared to pick up a pen at the wrong time or looked in the wrong direction, and the situation can quickly escalate. The truth is these children will grow into adults who will shape the world in which we live. What children see, they will learn, and what they experience, they carry with them. Connecting before correcting is not just a strategy; it is a fundamental principle in fostering belonging and behavioural development.

Let's talk about the children who arrive at school late. You see them walking towards the drive and you shout, 'Hurry up, you are late. Where have you been?' It's no wonder the child continues to be late and suffers poor attendance at school. Greeting on a level that engages a child – 'How was the football match at the weekend?' – prior to talking about the lateness, gets a much more positive response but also helps to ensure children belong. I once witnessed a headteacher berate a child at the school gates because his trousers were too short, telling them, 'I am providing the best teachers in the country for you. How dare you arrive in school with trousers like that!' Can you imagine being that child? Can you imagine how that must have felt?

There is always a reason sitting behind a child's behaviour. You will teach in schools that will have their own approach and expectations towards behaviour management; ensure this aligns with your own philosophy. Some schools will take a relational approach to behaviour, others will lean toward a more punitive model, and many will lie somewhere in between, but either way, you will not flourish in a school where there is a misalignment of values. The school with the headteacher barking at the gate at the child with the short trousers was not the school for me.

'Exclusion' is an ugly word; it carries connotations of isolation, rejection, disconnection – the list could go on. But why are children excluded? You will hear the language 'suspension' and 'permanent exclusion', but what are they? Permanent is as it states: the child can no longer attend the school they were permanently excluded from. Suspension is to suspend for a fixed period before reintegrating back into school. The complexities leaders face when making such decisions are multifaceted. The only person who can suspend or exclude is the headteacher.

Prior to looking at the reasons why a headteacher may decide to suspend or permanently exclude, it is important to understand the school environment must be safe for all; there must be clearly defined routines and understanding by all as to what is expected within the community. These foundations are integral to a safe and happy community. Within these expectations will be red lines, which indicate behaviours and actions that will not be tolerated. This could be children fighting or the possession or use of a prohibited item. Suspension could be used as a short-term measure of up to five consecutive days, a maximum of 15 in a term or 45 per academic year. There are many factors which will have to be considered when reaching a conclusion as to whether to suspend. Decisions are made on the balance of probability, and several things may need to be collected prior to making this decision, such as student and staff statements.

It is tempting to think that suspension resolves a problem. In the short term, it might: the pupil who swore at you isn't in your classroom tomorrow. But what then? Suspending a child often delays rather than addresses the root cause of the issue. It delays the process of repair, and it paints a further picture that the child does not belong; routines are broken, gaps are formed, and often the children who are more likely to be suspended are those who have additional needs or are disadvantaged, increasing the gap between them and their peers. Suspension must be followed by a reintegration meeting which works to understand the *why* and support the child to move forward. All too often, I have heard reintegration targets simply be a list of 'you must follow the rules' or 'you must be kind to others'; they often do not address the *how* or the *why*, and therefore the same behaviour occurs again.

Occasionally, it may be decided that, despite several interventions, a child needs a fresh start at a new school. It could come at the request of a parent or carer, or it could be instigated by the school. These are known as offsite directions (OSD). An OSD sets out to achieve one of two things:

- for the student to be successful over a 12-week period and offered a place to remain at the new school or
- to use as a short-term measure to see an improvement in behaviour and a return to their home school.

These work best when all stakeholders agree to the move, and often this can be when friendships and peers have a detrimental impact upon behaviour choices and a fresh start in a new school is needed. I have supported many OSDs both into and out of school, and they are successful when all agree that a change of environment is needed. Again, review meetings and regular contact and planning between the schools and families is vital for the placement to be successful.

OSDs for short-term behaviour improvement without the support of parents end up being 'done to', and the desire to engage from the outset is not there. Generally, these are not successful and tarnish relationships with both parents and the child. This gives the message of 'we do not want you'. I've seen this happen: when a student returns, often their behaviour deteriorates further and results in a permanent exclusion. The quick fix or easier option to place a student offsite stops the immediate issue, much the same as a suspension, but it does not address the underlying cause, instead covering it with a sticking plaster.

When it comes to permanent exclusion, these can be given for one of two reasons: persistent breaches of the school behaviour policy or a one-off serious breach, where allowing them to remain at the school would harm the education and welfare of others. This is a last resort and requires a pack of information to be served upon all stakeholders for the decision to be heard at a hearing, where the governing body will uphold the decision, agreeing the process has been a fair one, or will decide to reinstate the student. A situation known as the 'exclusion to prison pipeline' is widely reported. This is where exclusion from school removes protective factors around a child, exposing the child to a higher risk of exploitation and gang involvement. Couple this with the student who has additional needs or is disadvantaged, and the risk of vulnerability is heightened.

As adults, we must see the potential in all children, not just the problem. Really know the children you teach; understand their complexities and triggers. Be the person who doesn't give up on them and is relentless in establishing relationships. A strong leadership seeks to include rather than exclude, to restore rather than reject. Know that decisions are well thought through, and consideration of multiple factors is fundamental to the decision-making process. Be mindful that although temporarily removing a child from the classroom may give an immediate solution, it certainly does not support their return, nor does it support the child in the long run. In the classroom and beyond, your role is to create spaces where children feel they belong. Relationships are the foundation of learning; be relentless in building them.

Emma Dodds

Q What can pupil referral units and alternative provision teach us about behaviour?

A When reflecting upon behaviour and the best way to understand and support students, the question 'What can PRUs and alternative provision AP teach us?' is a great place to start. PRUs and AP often offer support and intervention when students hit crisis point in their educational journey, utilising a unique approach to understand a student's presentation while implementing the support needed to find a way forward. Increasingly, PRUs and AP are being commissioned to implement preventative work to avoid students reaching crisis point, guiding the referring school with recommendations and strategies to use. While there are many strategies that PRUs and AP can guide partners to when seeking to understand behaviour, the two expanded on below form a core foundation to build upon.

Be curious and never assume

If you look beyond behaviour being the *root cause* and see it as a symptom that evolves from the root, we can begin to open our minds to be curious about what may be happening for a student in school. If you assume we are seeing a behaviour because of choice, we close our minds to the possibility that a student may be exhibiting a behaviour because of an unmet or unidentified need. Increasingly, within our setting we are inducting key stage 4 pupils who cannot fluently read, who have masked this for many years through avoidance and hiding behind an outward presentation of behaviour as a coping mechanism. A curious approach to these 'behaviours' at an earlier age would have led to early identification and intervention while disrupting the all-too-frequent disenfranchisement that we see occur in these scenarios. So how would we be curious? A great place to start is reflecting as to what happened before the behaviour presented? What were the demands placed upon the student? What should they have been doing in that moment? These questions can guide us in remaining open-minded about what the function has been that was driving the behaviour.

A relational and restorative approach

Touching back on the 'root cause' of behaviour, it's important to remember this won't always be related to a learning need. Many students with SEMH needs present behaviours in the classroom with the function of distracting themselves from their inner thoughts or even creating predictability in an environment in which they don't feel safe and secure. Taking this into account, it is imperative that the classroom environment is one in which students have clear systems and routines that foster feelings of safety and security. If you can successfully partner this in your classroom with strong student relationships that are fostered through understanding, care, and curiosity, then you are mixing all the right ingredients to build a sense of belonging and connection with your students. When I talk about this topic, a student who we supported to return to mainstream education always comes to mind. After two very successful terms, we were contacted by the school after she was identified as again being at risk of permanent exclusion. One of our team went out to undertake some outreach work, and she readily shared that her aunt who supported her with her mother's care had recently passed away. The weight of now being the primary caregiver to her mother, coupled with her grief, had resulted in her expressing her emotions through her behaviour in school. A curious relational approach by the school in this scenario would have taken some pressure from this student, making her feel safe and cared for when she needed it the most.

While implementing a relational approach will reduce incidences of challenging behaviour, it won't guarantee that it will never happen, which is where the importance of a restorative approach comes into play. Using a restorative approach when incidents have taken place has a much greater impact than the use of punitive consequences.

Applying a restorative framework following conflict or when incidents have taken place can be far more successful in supporting students' understanding and learning than a punitive approach will achieve. Students who have experienced trauma or who have SEMH needs are more likely to be adversely affected by punitive sanctions, which compound feelings of shame and a sense of failure. By engaging in restorative interactions, students learn that relationships can last and are worth maintaining and repairing. Coupling this strongly with an embedded relational approach increases motivation and hope that every moment is an opportunity for a fresh start.

Zoe Johal

Q How can I effectively collaborate with colleagues and support staff to maintain a consistent approach to student behaviour?

A Research underscores that a collaborative, whole-school approach to behaviour management is significantly more effective than individual, isolated efforts (Kraft and Papay, 2014; Simonsen et al., 2010).

Consistency in behavioural expectations and responses across all staff members is a key determinant of effective behaviour management. Inconsistent approaches can confuse students and undermine both classroom authority and wider school norms (Sugai and Horner, 2009). Research by Simonsen et al. (2010) in their study on school-wide positive behaviour support found that schools implementing consistently applied behaviour expectations saw reductions in office discipline referrals and improvements in school climate. This reinforces the need for new teachers to align their practices with those of their colleagues and to seek clarity when in doubt. To do this, new teachers need a robust, shared mental model of the way we do things round here. Proactively ask, 'How do we typically respond to lateness or low-level disruption in this year group?' and adapt your approach accordingly. You may need to discuss this with expert colleagues.

Research also supports the view that peer collaboration enhances teacher efficacy and reduces stress, especially in early-career teachers. Kraft and Papay (2014) found that teachers working in schools with high levels of collegiality and shared instructional dialogue improved more over time than those in less collaborative settings. For new teachers, this means:

- Seeking mentorship or pairing with an experienced teacher to observe behaviour management routines.
- Participating in collaborative planning or debriefing sessions to reflect on behavioural strategies.
- Using staff meetings or year team discussions to align on approaches to issues like uniform, transitions, or praise systems.

Teaching assistants (TAs), pastoral staff, and special educational needs and disabilities (SEND) specialists also play a vital role in reinforcing consistent behavioural expectations. Research from Blatchford et al. (2012) highlights that effective deployment of support staff not only enhances student behaviour and inclusion but also eases the classroom burden on teachers, but only when communication is clear. Effective collaboration with support staff includes pre-lesson briefings to clarify expectations and share known triggers for individual pupils. Having a shared use of language around behaviour is also really useful, as is asking TAs for observations during lessons and acting on them. This shows that you value support staff and sends a message to students that you are a big team.

A consistent approach requires fidelity to school-wide systems, whether that's restorative conversations, behaviour tracking apps, or merit points. However, these tools only work if staff use them consistently and collectively. In a study of secondary schools with strong behaviour cultures, Tom Bennett (Department for Education, 2017) found that the schools most successful in managing behaviour had a clear system with shared responsibility and high levels of follow-through from all staff. Therefore, it is essential that new teachers learn the routines and follow through consistently, so students experience fairness. But new teachers should also not be afraid to escalate when necessary. The system only works when everyone plays their part. It might be useful to ask your mentor to walk you through a 'typical consequence pathway' for a scenario.

Effective collaboration also means being open to feedback and seeking advice. This aligns with the concept of relational trust (Bryk and Schneider, 2002), which is foundational to school improvement and staff cohesion. New teachers can build this trust by inviting colleagues to observe their routines and offer feedback, and also to be vulnerable too. For example, asking a colleague, 'Can I run a transition routine by you to see if it aligns with what we're doing across the corridor?'

New teachers are not just recipients of school culture. They are contributors to it. Research by Godfrey (2016) on collective efficacy in schools suggests that when staff believe in their collective ability to manage behaviour and maintain high standards, outcomes improve for all students. By aligning with colleagues, communicating with support staff, and reflecting on shared experiences, ECTs actively reinforce the school's behaviour ethos, building not only consistency but confidence.

Dr Haili Hughes

Q What does the local authority have to do with behaviour in my class?

A The local authority (LA) plays a multifaceted and crucial role in shaping and overseeing behaviour in schools, a role that is particularly relevant to our work as advocates for young people and families. While schools are largely autonomous in their day-to-day management of behaviour, the LA provides the overarching framework, guidance, and, at times, direct intervention that influences how behaviour is understood, addressed, and improved within their geographical area. Our success as young person and family champions, mediators, and proponents of inclusion hinges on a thorough understanding of this intricate relationship.

One of the LA's primary responsibilities is to ensure that all schools within its remit comply with statutory duties and national guidance related to behaviour and exclusion. This includes ensuring schools have robust behaviour policies in place, that these policies are accessible to parents, and that they align with DfE guidelines. The LA acts as a monitoring body, offering advice and support to schools to help them meet these expectations. When we, as advocates, encounter a situation where a school's behaviour policy seems unfair or inconsistent with national guidance, our knowledge of the LA's oversight role allows us to guide families in challenging these practices effectively, often by first engaging with the school, but escalating to the LA if necessary.

Beyond mere compliance, the LA often takes a proactive stance in promoting positive behaviour and inclusion across its schools. This can manifest in various ways, such as developing and disseminating best-practice guidance on behaviour management strategies, or offering training to school staff on topics like de-escalation techniques, restorative justice, or managing challenging behaviour. They may also commission specialist services that schools can access, such as educational psychology, emotional and mental health support, or behaviour support teams. These services are vital for schools grappling with complex behaviour issues that require a level of expertise beyond what general teaching staff may possess. For us, understanding the availability of these LA-commissioned services is key to signposting families and schools to appropriate support, ensuring that children's needs are met holistically rather than resorting to punitive measures.

Furthermore, the LA plays a significant role in the statutory process of school exclusions. While schools have the power to exclude pupils, the LA is responsible for reviewing all permanent exclusions and ensuring that due process has been followed. They also have a duty to arrange suitable alternative provision for excluded pupils from the sixth day of their exclusion. This is an area where our advocacy is often critical. We work closely with families facing exclusion, helping them understand their rights, challenging unjust decisions, and advocating for suitable alternative provision that meets the young person's needs and facilitates their reintegration into education. Our relationship with the LA's exclusion team is therefore paramount, as we often collaborate to achieve the best outcomes for excluded children.

Inclusion is a central tenet of our work, and the LA is instrumental in driving the inclusive agenda across its schools. This includes their responsibilities relating to pupils with SEND. The LA is responsible for identifying, assessing, and providing for children with SEND, which often involves complex behaviour needs. They coordinate the Education, Health, and Care (EHC) plan process, ensuring that appropriate provision is made to support these children to thrive in mainstream settings wherever possible. When a child's challenging behaviour stems from unmet SEND, our role as advocates often involves guiding families through the SEND identification process, advocating for specific provisions within an EHC plan, and working with the LA to ensure that schools implement these plans effectively.

Our trust-based relationships with both families and the LA's SEND teams are essential here to ensure timely and effective support.

The LA also acts as a strategic planner, identifying trends in school behaviour, areas of concern, and developing borough-wide initiatives to address these. This could involve targeted support for schools struggling with high rates of persistent absence, anti-bullying campaigns, or programmes promoting positive mental health and well-being. By understanding these broader LA initiatives, we can better align our advocacy efforts, ensuring that our interventions for individual families contribute to the wider goals of the local educational system. This strategic awareness also helps us build and maintain our reputation and healthy relationships with schools and the community, demonstrating that our work is not just about individual cases, but about contributing to a more supportive and inclusive educational environment for all.

Finally, the LA often serves as a point of last resort for complaints that cannot be resolved at the school level. While our primary aim is to mediate and resolve issues directly between families and schools, there are occasions where this is not possible, or where a school's actions are consistently problematic. In such instances, guiding families on how to escalate their concerns to the LA, or even making representations to the LA ourselves, can be a necessary step.

Our deep understanding of the LA's responsibilities and processes allows us to navigate these situations effectively, ensuring that families have every avenue explored to achieve a fair resolution.

In summary, the LA's involvement in school behaviour is extensive, encompassing statutory oversight, proactive support, specialist provision, exclusion management, and a strong drive for inclusion, particularly for children with SEND. For us, as young person and family champions, understanding and effectively engaging with the LA is not merely an administrative exercise; it is fundamental to our ability to advocate effectively, mediate constructively, and build the trusting relationships that are the bedrock of our success in fostering a truly inclusive and supportive educational system for all young people.

Mervin Cato

Reflective questions

- How do my behaviour strategies align with the wider culture and ethos of my school?
- In what ways can I build stronger collaboration with colleagues and support staff?
- What invisible structures or systems in my school do I need to understand better?
- How can I contribute positively to shaping the culture beyond my own classroom?

References

Blatchford, P., Webster, R., and Russell, A. (2012) 'Challenging the role and deployment of teaching assistants in mainstream schools: The impact on student engagement.' *School Leadership & Management*, 32(1), pp. 3–20.

Bryk, A. S. and Schneider, B. (2002) *Trust in Schools: A Core Resource for Improvement*. Russell Sage Foundation.

Cramond, J. A. (2021) 'Teachers' and students' experiences of positive relationships in secondary education.' Newcastle University. Available at: https://theses.ncl.ac.uk/jspui/bitstream/10443/5400/1/Cramond%20J%20A%202021.pdf

Department for Education (DfE). (2017) *Creating a Culture: How school leaders can optimise behaviour*. Available at: https://assets.publishing.service.gov.uk/media/5a7506e4ed915d3c7d529cec/Tom_Bennett_Independent_Review_of_Behaviour_in_Schools.pdf

Education Endowment Foundation. (2019) *Improving Behaviour in Schools: Guidance Report*. Available at: https://educationendowmentfoundation.org.uk/education-evidence/guidance-reports/behaviour

Godfrey, D. (2016) 'Leadership of schools as research-led organisations in the English educational environment: Cultivating a research-engaged school culture.' *Educational Management Administration & Leadership*, 44(2), pp. 301–321.

Handy, C. (1990) *Understanding Schools as Organisations*. London: Penguin.

Handy, C. (1999) *Inside Organisations: 21 Ideas for Managers*. London: Penguin.

Kraft, M. A. and Papay, J. P. (2014) 'Can professional environments in schools promote teacher development?' *Educational Evaluation and Policy Analysis*, 36(4), pp. 476–500.

Simonsen, B., Fairbanks, S., Briesch, A., Myers, D., & Sugai, G. (2010) 'Evidence-based practices in classroom management: Considerations for research to practice.' *Education and Treatment of Children*, 33(3), pp. 351–380.

Starkey, J. (2023) 'Effective strategies for building and sustaining a positive school culture and climate.' *Academy of Educational Leadership Journal*, 27(S2), pp. 1–3.

Sugai, G. and Horner, R. H. (2009) 'Responsiveness-to-intervention and school-wide positive behavior supports: Integration of multi-tiered system approaches.' *Exceptionality*, 17(4), pp. 223–237.

4

Classrooms, conflict, and creating a culture of safety

In every classroom, behaviour is shaped by far more than individual choices. It is influenced by relationships, routines, curriculum design, physical space, teaching quality, and the wider culture of the school. Seating plans, transitions, corridor norms, peer dynamics, adult language, and leadership values all play a role in how behaviour emerges and how safe children feel. As an Early Career Teacher (ECT), your role is not simply to *manage* or *observe* behaviour, but to create the conditions in which all children can feel safe, seen, and supported. Across the chapter, safety is explored not only through relationships and regulation, but also through clarity, structure, and deliberate teaching.

This chapter brings together multiple, interconnected perspectives on behaviour, drawing on the expertise of teachers, leaders, and researchers across the key phases. Taking these perspectives together, these contributions move behaviour away from simplistic ideas of control and compliance, and towards a richer understanding of behaviour as relational, contextual, and connected to teaching, design, and culture.

The chapter begins by grounding behaviour in emotional safety, safeguarding, and inclusion. **Krupa Patel** offers two complementary

DOI: 10.4324/9781003592426-4

contributions that explore how teachers can respond to conflict and behaviour in ways that protect both emotional and physical wellbeing. Drawing on trauma-informed practice, restorative approaches, and safeguarding principles, Krupa supports ECTs to see behaviour as communication rather than defiance. She provides practical strategies for de-escalation, conflict resolution, and reflective practice, while also challenging teachers to think critically about how behaviour policies are implemented, lived, and experienced by children.

Alongside this, **Dr Sue Allingham** invites us to look backwards and forwards through the lens of the Early Years. Her contribution reminds us that the statutory duty to support, understand, and manage behaviour begins long before formal schooling, and that early experiences of regulation, belonging, and curriculum flexibility have lasting consequences. By drawing on Early Years practice and the work of Maria Montessori, Sue challenges behaviour systems that prioritise control over understanding, and asks ECTs to reflect on what we can learn from approaches rooted in co-regulation, emotional security, and developmentally appropriate expectations.

The chapter then widens its focus to consider the classroom as a physical and social environment. **Enzo Vullo** explores how design choices, layout, and use of space can actively contribute to a culture of safety. His work highlights how classrooms are not neutral containers but environments that can either reduce anxiety and friction or unintentionally heighten stress and dysregulation. This is followed by a strong emphasis on the social nature of behaviour: children do not behave in isolation; they behave in groups.

Philip Salisbury contributes across two sections of the chapter, bringing a grounded and relational perspective on behaviour, teaching, and organisation. He explores how good teaching reduces the conditions in which low-level disruption thrives, and how clarity, structure, and well-pitched learning support calm, purposeful classrooms. Philip also examines grouping and seating arrangements, offering practical, experience-led guidance on how classroom organisation can either support focus and inclusion or create unnecessary distraction and behavioural challenges.

David Didau's contributions focus sharply on classroom culture, routines, and teacher agency. He explores how ECTs can establish positive classroom cultures even when wider systems feel inconsistent or underdeveloped. Through practical guidance on routines, participation, visibility of thinking, and fair responses to collective behaviour, David reinforces the idea that culture is built deliberately, minute by minute and moment by moment. His sections emphasise that good behaviour is not simply the absence of noise or chaos, but the presence of attention, clarity, and shared expectations.

Finally, **Richard Clutterbuck** brings a leadership-informed lens to some of the most complex and sensitive aspects of classroom behaviour. His contributions examine what happens when behaviour starts to slip, when banter crosses into harm, and when issues such as misogyny emerge in the classrooms. Richard is clear that teachers cannot tackle these challenges alone: classroom culture is inseparable from the whole-school culture. Through practical scripts, examples, and reflections, he shows how values-led leadership, consistency, and adult alignment create the conditions in which teachers are empowered to challenge harmful behaviour safely and effectively.

Taken together, this chapter presents behaviour not as a checklist of strategies, but as a culture to be cultivated. When safeguarding is embedded, teaching is strong, routines are clear, spaces are thoughtfully designed, and values are consistently modelled, classrooms become places where learning can flourish. For ECTs, this chapter offers both reassurance and challenge: you are not responsible for everything, but what you do in your classroom matters deeply. In creating safety, clarity, and connection, you lay the foundations for behaviour that supports learning, dignity, and belonging for all.

Q How do I handle conflicts between students in a way that promotes inclusion?

A In answering this question, I look at how you, as an ECT, can respond to conflict in a way that builds connection, inclusion, and collective wellbeing. Conflict is inevitable; it is in all walks of life, but especially in the classroom, where multiple identities, emotions, intersections, and lived experiences come together in one space. The way we respond matters. When handled with empathy and curiosity, conflict offers powerful opportunities for learning, reflection, and growth.

Safety first – physical and emotional

Before we can talk about conflict resolution, we must prioritise safety. Physical and emotional safety are the foundations of any inclusive response. As a teacher, it's important to be aware of your physical environment. Know where the exits are, be mindful of sharp or heavy objects in the room, and think proactively about how you would respond if a situation escalates. If a conflict becomes volatile, you may need to calmly relocate the rest of the class to a safe space to reduce stimulation and protect all involved.

Use calm, minimal language like 'stop' or 'walk with me' to de-escalate where possible. If trained staff are available, deploy them and follow your setting's agreed plan. Swap out rather than pile in. Your composure – your breathing, tone, and body language – can be the regulation cue your students need.

Creating space for restorative practice

Restorative practice is not just a strategy – it's a mindset. When embedded in your school's behaviour policy, it offers a structured, relational way of repairing harm and rebuilding trust. These conversations centre on key questions, often including:

- What happened?
- How did that make you feel?

- How do you think the other person felt?
- What needs to happen to repair this?

This process supports accountability and mutual understanding, helping young people move from reaction to reflection. It's not about blame – it's about creating the conditions for emotional repair.

Thinking points

- Do you have a set of restorative questions available and accessible in your classroom? Could your students use these independently with adult scaffolding?

Modelling listening, reducing blame, and practising self-awareness

Active listening is a key tool when working through conflict, but it's not always easy – especially in the heat of the moment. Begin by creating time and space for all involved to regulate before initiating restorative dialogue. Model fairness by listening attentively to each student's account, using paraphrasing to reflect back what you've heard, and maintaining a calm, open demeanour.

Avoid using blame-laden language or threats – statements like 'Let's see what your mum says' can inflame feelings of shame or escalate emotions. Instead, try something like 'I can see this is really hard for you', which offers empathy while gently holding the boundary.

At the same time, keep checking in with yourself. What are your own triggers? What assumptions might you be holding? Practising self-awareness helps you remain grounded and solution-focused, and your students will notice and learn from your example.

Understand the 'why'

Conflicts often have roots deeper than what we see on the surface. A moment of anger or defiance might be linked to home stress, sensory overload, unmet needs, poor sleep, or previous trauma. Aim to listen with the intention to understand, not just to respond.

When students feel heard, they are more likely to participate in resolving the conflict meaningfully. This is where the deeper learning happens, when they begin to understand the impact of their actions, how to take responsibility, and how to begin repairing relationships in ways that feel authentic and manageable.

Encourage your students to identify their own triggers and reflect on how they can regulate before things escalate again. Support them to create their own solutions and actions for moving forward. Ownership empowers change.

Addressing power imbalances through transparency

Sometimes, conflict stems from perceived or actual power imbalances – among students or between adults and students. Be mindful of how privilege, bias, or unspoken hierarchies may shape a situation. Inclusion starts with trust, and trust requires transparency. Ensure that all voices are heard with equity, that no one feels sidelined or dismissed, and that your role remains facilitative rather than authoritarian.

Avoid making assumptions about who is 'in the wrong' or who 'always behaves like this'. These narratives can be limiting and harmful. Instead, show students that you are open to understanding their perspective and that you are committed to fairness, even when it's hard.

Practical strategies to support inclusive conflict resolution

- Co-produce restorative questions with students – they'll engage more meaningfully with language they've helped shape.
- Use cooperative learning structures to promote mutual accountability, shared goals, and interpersonal skills (Johnson & Johnson, 1989).
- Offer focus groups or discussion circles for students to share perspectives and foster understanding.

- Model real-life scenarios through role play and case studies to build emotional insight.
- Use safe words or signals students can use when they need a break or are reaching emotional overload.
- Set ground rules for all discussions – especially those involving conflict. Respectful communication must be a shared expectation.
- Take time to reflect. What are you learning about your students? About yourself? What patterns do you notice? Reflection supports future planning.

Inclusion through connection

Conflict is not a failure; it is part of human interaction. When we hold space for young people to reflect, repair, and reconnect, we nurture a culture of inclusion and psychological safety. Your job is not to have all the answers, but to be a steady presence that models fairness, curiosity, and emotional regulation.

In every conflict you navigate, there's an opportunity to model empathy, to reinforce boundaries, to build trust, and to create change. So pause, breathe, and remember: how you handle conflict sets the emotional tone for your classroom, and that tone has the power to shift everything.

Krupa Patel

Q What should I consider when implementing behaviour policies to ensure that students' emotional and physical wellbeing are protected?

A As an ECT, it's important to reflect on your role within the wider safeguarding and behaviour framework – particularly Standards 7 and 8 of the Teachers' Standards, which focus on managing behaviour and upholding professional behaviours. While all schools will have policies shaped by statutory guidance and legislation, safeguarding must be seen as more than just a policy. It is the foundation on which school culture is built, influencing every decision, operation, and holistic growth. At its heart, safeguarding is about creating the conditions where every child feels seen, safe, and supported.

When implementing behaviour policies that genuinely protect emotional and physical wellbeing, several key considerations must be taken into account. This question explores how to align your actions with these values, ensuring your behaviour management practices are inclusive, reflective, and rooted in care.

Think about stakeholders and communicate clearly

Safeguarding is everyone's responsibility. Ensuring effective implementation of behaviour policies requires collaboration with all key stakeholders: families, colleagues, governors, local agencies, and – most importantly – young people. Policies can't exist in isolation; they must reflect the realities and demographics of your school community.

Clear, open communication builds trust and ensures everyone understands how the policies are applied. Regular updates to related documents – such as the behaviour policy, Relationships and Sex Education (RSE) guidance, and the staff code of conduct – help maintain alignment and shared expectations.

For learners, the way in which the behaviour policy is communicated can make all the difference. Children must be given opportunities to ask questions, offer feedback, and understand the purpose behind the rules. Empowering them with this understanding promotes agency and strengthens emotional safety.

Thinking points

- What are the key demographics and needs of your community?
- How could you make the behaviour policy more accessible (e.g. visual summaries, translated versions, flow charts, or short videos for families, students, governors, and Ofsted)?

Engage in CPD

Effective implementation of CPD doesn't happen by accident; it must be intentional, measured, and consistent. The Education Endowment Foundation's implementation guidance (EEF, 2019) emphasises that professional development should be iterative and focused on embedding long-term change. As an ECT, you might wonder why I am including CPD in considering behaviour and strategies. The reality is, without your active engagement and reflection in CPD, you will be doing yourself and your professional lens a disservice.

When you are thinking about your training and the options available to you, consider how you can engage with training that is proactive, not reactive, as well as strategies that are aligned with your school's ethos. These may include restorative practice, trauma-informed approaches, CALM (Crisis Aggression Limitation and Management) de-escalation techniques, zones of regulation, or positive behaviour support. These approaches help staff understand behaviour from the broader perspective and respond with curiosity, not control.

CPD should not be seen as a one-off event, but an ongoing process of learning, reflection, and adaptation. When training is embedded into staff culture, it supports consistency and compassion across the whole school community (Hobson and Malderez, 2013). As an ECT, you create as well as respond to that school culture.

Consistency and fairness build trust

Children feel safer when expectations are applied fairly and consistently. They're quick to notice when certain students are treated differently or when rules are inconsistently enforced. This can erode trust and contribute to feelings of injustice.

To foster equity, reflect on your own practice. How do your actions align with school policies? Are you applying rules with empathy, while also holding boundaries? Equitable behaviour management does not mean treating every child the same; it means recognising individual need while maintaining high expectations for all.

Staff training should also include time to reflect on unconscious bias, triangulate evidence, and use data to inform decisions. Consistency isn't about rigidity; it's about reliability.

Thinking points

- Are the procedures clear and consistently applied?
- Are proactive, preventative approaches embedded in practice?
- Do communication strategies include calm de-escalation cues (e.g. break cards, silence, short sentences)?
- Are you regularly observing what students are *showing*, not just what they are *saying*?

Reframe behaviour as communication

When we understand that behaviour often signals unmet needs, we become more responsive and less reactive. Students may act out not because they are defiant but because they are dysregulated, confused, or overwhelmed. Rather than rushing to impose consequences, begin by observing and listening.

Restorative practices offer a way to respond to these moments with empathy and structure. Rather than focusing on punishment, they invite reflection, accountability, and repair. Remember that emotional and cognitive maturity does not always align with age, especially in children with trauma histories or SEND. Big behaviours are often signs of vulnerability, not defiance.

For restorative approaches to be effective, they must be embedded in a whole-school culture and supported by clear systems that allow time and space for reflection and relationship repair.

Create space and time for student voice

Schools that truly listen to students are schools that learn. A high volume of student feedback, whether positive or challenging, is not a sign of dysfunction but a sign of psychological safety. When young people feel safe, they speak up.

To support this, offer multiple ways for students to share their views: class meetings, circle time, mentoring check-ins, suggestion boxes, creative expression, and anonymous surveys. Some may feel confident in group discussions; others may need quieter, more private methods. What matters is that the door is open – and kept open.

Listening to students isn't just a nice idea; it is a vital part of evaluating whether behaviour policies are working. Their voices reveal gaps, patterns, and potential improvements. As Ofsted (2023) highlights, student engagement is strongest when young people are involved in shaping their environments.

Reflect and evaluate behaviour policies regularly

Regular evaluations ensure they remain relevant and include any changing dynamics. Schools and communities are constantly changing, and policies must evolve with them. Ongoing evaluation ensures that policies remain relevant, inclusive, and effective.

Use behaviour data not just to track incidents but to look for patterns and tell stories. Are certain groups disproportionately affected by sanctions? Where are rewards being applied – and are they meaningful to students? Combine data with lived experiences to inform decision making and ensure the policy remains grounded in reality. Kolb's (1984) experiential learning model reminds us that reflection leads to insight, and insight leads to improvement. That cycle – observe, reflect, adapt – is central to keeping safeguarding alive and responsive.

In summary

Implementing behaviour policies in a way that protects students' emotional and physical wellbeing isn't just about following procedures; it's about embedding a mindset of care, consistency, and co-creation. When behaviour strategies are aligned with the school's values, when students and families are actively included, and when staff are supported through meaningful CPD and reflection, schools become places of safety and growth for all.

This section offers reflection points and prompts you can take back to your teams, questions that open up conversations about the heart of your school's policies and how they live in day-to-day practice. A behaviour policy should not be a document gathering dust; it should be a lived, shared, and evolving strategy that helps every child feel safe, supported, and seen.

Krupa Patel

Q What can we learn from the Early Years about 'behaviour'?

A In the Early Years Foundation Stage Statutory Framework (2025), there is a section that is entitled 'Supporting and understanding children's behaviour'. At first glance, this sounds as if it will be useful and informative. However, as the section goes on, it becomes clear that this is not the case. Section 3.73 states, 'Providers are responsible for supporting, understanding, and managing children's behaviour in an appropriate way', and section 3.74 goes on to explain that 'Providers must not give or threaten corporal punishment or any punishment which could negatively affect a child's well-being'.

We have a statutory duty to support, understand, and manage behaviour obviously in a non-threatening way, but with no guidance as to how to go about it. So it is of no surprise that such things as rewards, points, behaviour charts, marble jars and 'golden time' are still often suggested as ways to 'manage behaviour' in Early Childhood Education and Care (ECEC).

When 'behaviour' is spoken of and seen as something to be 'managed', a particular negative spin is put upon it. Therefore, it is vital that we notice and reflect on the words that precede 'managing'. If we reflect on the words 'supporting' and 'understanding', then we are obliged to go deeper into the causes and meanings behind the way children behave. This means that we have to take seriously the statement 'all behaviour is communication'. The youngest children are still finding out about the world and their place within it. Much will happen to them that they do not yet understand or know how to deal with. This can be frightening and overwhelming, and the feelings may well overcome children in ways that they cannot yet control. At this point, we must avoid judgements so that we can adopt the role of co-regulator, supporting and guiding the children to manage their feelings and behaviour and move towards being able to self-regulate.

Children want to be able to feel they belong, but it is not always easy for them to fit in because they find themselves in an unfamiliar situation or environment. With so little life experience, the youngest children may not yet have the life skills or knowledge to navigate such a situation. Their emotions may well manifest in ways that adults may not approve of or feel comfortable with. Hence the use of behaviour charts and the other artificial constructs mentioned previously.

It is for skilled educators who take on the statutory role of key person (someone who understands the child) to create an emotional and physical environment that supports an enabling and secure environment in which children who become dysregulated can feel safe. An important question to ourselves is 'How well do I know this child/these children?' How is what I am expecting of them suiting what I know?

In 1912, Maria Montessori noticed that a rigid curriculum has an impact on behaviour:

> We know only too well the sorry spectacle of the teacher who, in the ordinary schoolroom, must pour certain cut and dried facts into the heads of the scholars. In order to succeed in this barren

> task, she finds it necessary to discipline her pupils into immobility and to force their attention. Prizes and punishments are ever-ready and efficient aids to the master who must force into a given attitude of mind and body those who are condemned to be his listeners.
>
> (Montessori, 1964, p.21)

I would argue that this is true in ECEC and beyond. Up to an hour of phonics and sitting still the minute a reception child arrives in school is not conducive to good 'behaviour' and sets up difficult relationships and expectations that project into the future. The statutory requirement of the Early Years Foundation Stage (EYFS) that we support, understand, and manage behaviour must provide food for thought and action into Key Stage 1 and beyond.

Dr Sue Allingham

Q How can I create a culture of safety and certainty through design?

A Supporting pupils with additional social, emotional, and mental health (SEMH) needs is a challenging task. The type of need is wide and often complex, which makes managing a classroom and learning difficult.

The very act of learning requires a leaner to be challenged and pushed outside of their comfort zone; it also requires an individual to fail, receive feedback, and then apply that feedback.

A pupil with additional SEMH needs will find this process a challenge as they will operate from a position of emotional flooding, where they walk through life at a 7 out of 10. Any spike in emotion will push they to a '10', which results in involuntary dysregulation and, for many pupils in alternative educational settings, undesirable behaviours that requires adult support.

If the SEMH need is driven by trauma, then the act of 'a failing' when working through the process of learning could take them back to the trauma – for example, children that are victims of physical abuse could associate failing with physical hurt.

The answer to this is simple: make the pupils feel safe. The execution of this is more complex, but achievable.

To support leaners with additional SEMH needs, at GROW Harlow, the SEMH provision I run, I ensure the environment is built to create a culture of safety, through certainty.

If a learner skirts around the edge of emotional dysregulation through their day, the introduction of certainty in an environment can bring them down to a level where adults can co-regulate with them and pupils can apply the self-regulation tools and approaches taught to them.

I approach environment as two things: the physical environment (the setting) and the emotional environment (the pupil's reaction to instructions).

The physical environment provides an opportunity to get ahead of any potential spikes in emotion for the pupil. The questions I would ask myself relate to giving the pupil the best possible chance of making the right choices.

I start with ensuring the learning environment is clean and clutter-free, and provides a low sensory stimulus (think about colours, smells, direct sunlight, etc.).

Next, I think about the learning journey I want the pupil to go through in the session. Can they see what I want them to see? Can they hear what I want them to hear? Can they move how I want them to move? Can they think? What are the potential areas of friction for the children? I think it is important to consider the additional needs of the child here also. For example, many children I support need glasses but refuse to wear them – so I must take responsibility for them being able to see without their glasses.

I also think about the certainty of what is happening throughout the day. I like the use of visual timetables *but* they must be accessible so that they can be viewed and referenced by the children. I like to have a visual timetable in the different rooms of GROW Harlow. I also like the visual timetable to go left to right, as when reading, as this allow pupils to 'walk' the day if they wish.

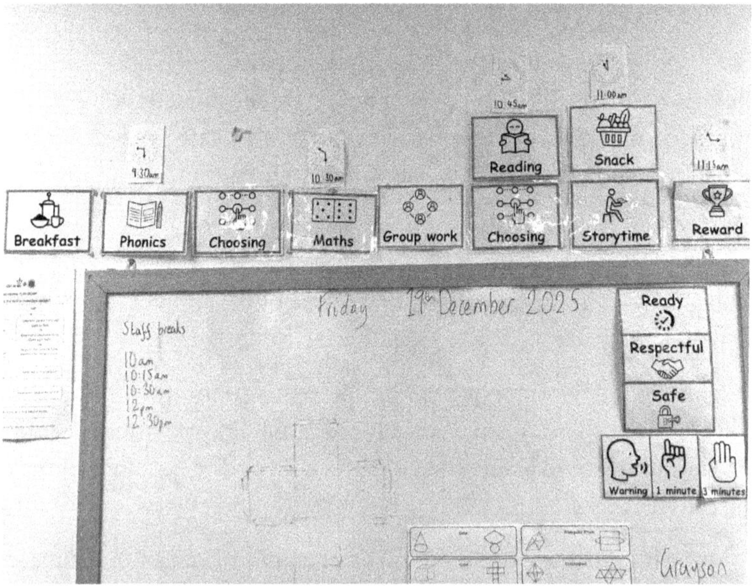

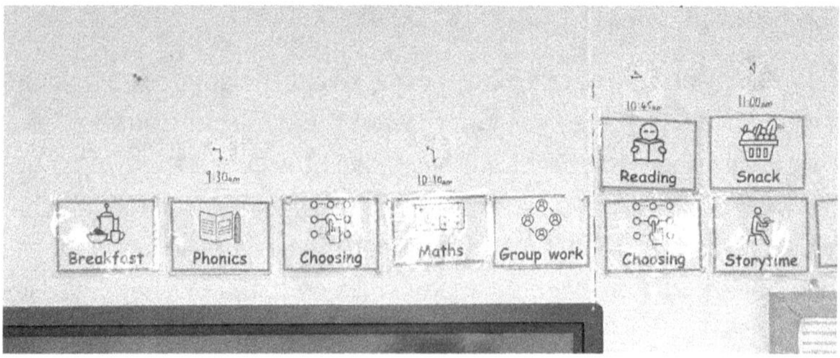

Physical cues are also important to scaffold protocols and rule-following to help children with additional SEMH needs to make 'good' choices.

In the image below, you can see lines on the floor. This is for lining up when we transition between rooms. This is important to support the pupil's decision making – they must stand behind the line, with their voices off. Very simple.

This familiarity of the use of lines then can be applied to be used in other activities. In the following image, you can see the use of lines as a safety precaution when roasting marshmallows.

This certainty promotes safety – the pupil understands and is experienced with the rules around waiting behind a line. When this is introduced to a 'high excitement' activity, such as independently roasting marshmallows, emotion and cognitive load is not spiked further by the requirement to follow a new, unfamiliar, rule, which also could raise the stakes of the pupil thinking that if they do not follow the rule, they will not be able to a take part in the activity.

All physical cues need to be applied consistently, as they are linked to the 'emotional environment', the other part of creating a culture of safety through design.

A pupil with additional SEMH needs will require the certainty of knowing how you will react. Ideally, all adults and staff will always remain regulated; if not, they should be able to step out of the setting to self-regulate.

Behaviour is communication. Regulated adults communicate that they are in control and able to keep the pupil safe.

I combine this with a physical cue – I wear the same clothes every day. I appreciate that this is overkill, but it demonstrates a point to the pupils – you will get the same from me every day.

A real-life example of a pupil knowing how I will react and feeling safe enough to allow me to support them was when I was transitioning a pupil back to mainstream. The pupil was in their mainstream classroom; I was on site with him, but in the toilet. On the leaving the toilet, I was confronted by the headteacher. They told me the pupil had run out of the classroom and was in the dining hall, standing on a table and refusing to get down. I walked into the dining hall and asked the pupil to get down from the table. He did so. I then asked him what the issue was. He said that the maths was different. I said, 'Okay, come with me and let's go fix this.' He then followed me back to the classroom, and after a quick adjustment, he completed the maths work. The headteacher asked me to write down the 'script' I had used. I explained that it wasn't about a script; it was about me following through and over-communicating with him through the six-month placement at GROW Harlow, which resulted in him feeling safe to follow my instructions as he knew nothing 'bad' would happen to him. Did we have challenging situations during his placement? Yes. Did I have to sanction him? Yes. But every time, I approached the situation in a regulated and transparent way. He knew the rules, and he knew the consequences. There were no surprises.

There is much to think about as an ECT. Be kind to yourself. Think about what outcome you want, and approach the setup of your physical environment to give the pupils the best chance to succeed. Relationships matter, as do the clarity and consistency of your verbal and non-verbal communication.

The most exciting thing about designing your approaches for safety is that all the children will benefit, as will you.

Enzo Vullo

Q What does teaching have to do with behaviour?

A Not all bad behaviour is down to bad teaching, although in my experience good teaching can eliminate many low-level bad behaviours. Good behaviour starts on the first day and in the first moment the child enters your classroom. I have discussed previously how essential it is that children are greeted and presented with meaningful activities as soon as they enter the classroom. Acknowledging children when they enter, being organised with resources and plans, and creating a positive purposeful environment are all essential in creating good learning conditions.

Good teaching helps to eliminate bad behaviour because it removes the conditions in which low-level disruption becomes an issue. Having well-planned lessons that are adapted to meet the needs of individual children and are inherently challenging for all children is essential. Shaping and framing tasks that cater for individual needs will ensure that all children can achieve. It is my firm belief that poor behaviour in classrooms can be improved through good teaching. In primary schools, it is extremely rare for children to decide to behave badly for no reason. Children also very rarely decide to deliberately do things wrong. Sometimes breaking down tasks, giving individual instruction, checking in with individual pupils and adapting those tasks can all help to eradicate bad behaviour. If children have a task they can do and they are given the tools to do it, they will almost always get on with it. This is why clear instruction modelling and effective questioning techniques (either to assess understanding or correct misconceptions) are so important. In classrooms where teaching is poor, behaviour is inevitably worse. Misguided tasks, confused explanations, work pitched inappropriately, and work that does not build on previous learning will all contribute to poor behaviour. That is why good teaching is so essential. Understanding that the curriculum is a continuum and knowing where individual children are on that line is really important. I would advise any new teacher to read the Rosenshine principles and look at the work of Tom Sherrington. (See, for example, Sherrington, 2019).

Finally, in my experience, intrinsic motivation is the biggest single driving force for pupils. Having a sense of achievement, understanding, and seeing the progress that they're making (what they're getting better at) will motivate pupils and improve behaviour. If you can create a classroom that is calm and purposeful and creates the right conditions for every child to learn, you are on your way to being an exceptional teacher.

Philip Salisbury

Q How do I create a positive classroom culture?

A As an ECT, you don't control the timetable, the corridor policy, or the detention system – yet. You *do* control a few square metres of carpet and sixty minutes of students' attention. In that space, you set the tone and can establish a norm in which everyone participates. You decide how thinking is checked, and you choose whether routines are taught or assumed. Culture doesn't trickle down to you; it radiates out from you. This is where we all start.

1. Behaviour first, always

In too many classrooms, teachers are forced to battle for attention. In these environments, talk of sparking curiosity or connecting learning to the wider world feels almost cruel. When you're spending every lesson trying to get children to sit down, be quiet, and do as they're asked, you're hardly in a position to make space for discussion or to model intellectual wonder. Good behaviour is not a nice-to-have: it's the bedrock on which everything else rests.

It is often a tacit agreement in classrooms that if the teacher agrees not to bother the students, they agree not to be difficult. When teachers expect students to participate, they are often met with bewildered hostility. In some schools, students are routinely given active permission not to participate in the form of out-of-lesson passes or instructions to teachers that they should not be ask a question. This makes any kind of engaging approach to teaching untenable.

Good schools are ones in which teachers are supported to build a classroom culture in which children are expected to participate. You know that this is happening because these schools are full of classrooms in which it's normal for teachers to ask all students to answer questions using mini-whiteboard routines, where there are regular paired discussions to check that all students understand what has been taught, where students are expected to listen to the teacher and each other. None of these things is hard to do in schools with good behaviour, but they are an uphill struggle in schools where the established culture is to opt out.

- **Silent start:** Greet at the door; a short 'Do Now' on the board. No admin chat. Pens moving within 30 seconds.
- **Attention signal:** One signal, practised. 'Track me.' Then mean it.
- **Teach routines:** Narrate compliance, apply consequences calmly, and move on. Sanctions should be certain, never severe.
- **Participation is required:** Make 'opt out' harder than joining in. The norm is 'Everyone thinks; everyone shares'.

Good behaviour isn't the absence of noise; it's the presence of attention. You can't spark curiosity in a gale.

2. Make thinking visible (to you and to them)

I still meet classes where no one is asked anything. Information is told, tasks are set, mistakes are corrected, but no one checks whether anyone *understood.* Don't guess what students might be thinking; sample constantly.

- **Mini-whiteboards** every 2–3 minutes: a definition, a worked step, a retrieval item. 'Show me.' Scan the room; reteach *now*, not next week.
- **Cold call** (warmly): ask the question, *pause*, then name the student. Build the habit that anyone might be asked because everyone is *thinking*.
- **Pair talk with purpose:** 20–40 seconds, a precise prompt, then a targeted share-out.
- **Wait time** that allows all students – especially those that need time – to think. Too often, teachers ask a question and expect an answer in less than a second.

When students know their thinking will be made visible, they attend. When you know what they're thinking, you can teach effectively.

3. Build dignity through success

A positive culture is not vibes and posters; it's the lived experience of doing demanding work successfully.

- **Right-sized challenge:** If it's too easy, attention wanders; too hard, effort collapses. Pitch high, scaffold tightly.
- **Success before struggle:** Model first, then guided practice, then independent application.
- **Public excellence, private correction:** Put great work under the visualiser; give sensitive feedback quietly.

Students feel valued when their effort reliably leads somewhere worth arriving.

Positive classroom culture is simple, not easy: clear norms, visible thinking, deliberate preparation, coherent curriculum, and adult trust. You make the weather in your room. Leaders set the climate. Start today: teach the routines, see the thinking, and let success do the heavy lifting.

David Didau

Q What do I do when the rest of the class starts copying negative behaviour?

A One of the worst lessons I experienced during my first year of teaching started with a hum. One student, barely audible. I paused mid-sentence, scanned the room. I couldn't tell who it was – everyone was innocent-faced. Then another joined in. Then another. Within moments, the room vibrated with a low, defiant buzz. Not quite singing, not quite talking, just enough to irritate and destabilise. It was the auditory equivalent of being pecked to death by sparrows.

I lost it. 'Right! Since you all think this is so funny, you can all stay behind.'

And just like that, I handed them the moral high ground. The problem with collective punishment is that it punishes the innocent along with the guilty. When you tell a class, 'If one more person talks, no one's going to lunch', you shift the dynamic. Now, instead of seeing you as the adult trying to maintain order, they see you as the tyrant dishing out unfairness. You galvanise the whole group *against* you, rather than working with those who want to learn. Worst of all, you remove agency. If they're going to get punished anyway, why *not* misbehave?

What I should have done is what I do now. As soon as I hear that first hum (or whatever silliness it is), I don't react – I act. Clipboard in hand, seating plan at the ready, I walk. I write. Quietly, methodically. Not to shame, not to scold, but to show that I've noticed and that I'll follow up. There's a strange magic to silent logging. It says: I'm calm, I'm in control, I will not be thrown off course.

Before the next lesson, I'll catch the ringleader at the door. 'Last time, you chose to [insert daft behaviour here]. That made it harder for others to focus. Today, I'll be watching to see if you can stay on task.' It's private, calm, and positively framed. No drama, no lecture, just a quiet reminder that they're capable of doing better and that you're paying attention. You're not dragging the past into the room; you're pointing towards a better version of the lesson and of them.

When the behaviour becomes contagious, it's tempting to punish everyone. Don't. Always be proportionate. Students are exquisitely attuned to injustice. If your response feels excessive, you undermine your authority. Instead, pause the lesson. 'This isn't working. We need to reset.' Then go back to basics. Reteach entry routines. Re-establish silence. It might feel like going backwards, but it's how you move forward.

Whenever I've seen frustrated teachers deploy collective punishment, it's usually a last, desperate act. The most frustrating part is that it's actually very easy to avoid. Here follows my very simple solution to dealing with unidentified troublemakers in a way that doesn't punish the compliant.

First, you *know* who they are. You might not have caught them in the act, you might not be able to prove it beyond reasonable doubt, but you *know*. After all, they've got form. You also know who is without sin. Some children *never* misbehave, whatever the provocation. It is never fair or acceptable to punish these poor, put-upon kids.

On those occasions (and there have been many) when I had to write minutes on the board to persuade errant pupils to follow basic instructions, when the end of the lesson came, I would let the innocent go. Everyone would be made to stand quietly behind their desks and those I knew to be pure at heart would be allowed to leave. I would then launch into some variant of my 'disappointed' lecture. At this point there would be some pupils who tried the line 'But it wasn't me' or 'But I wasn't as bad as Tom'. In response, I would either say, 'Well, it is now' or 'I know that, and the sooner I've finished speaking, the sooner you will go and I will be able to speak to Tom privately'. Now, the next layer of minor miscreants can be released. They might not have done much, and they might not have been involved *this particular time*, and you have shown you realise they are not the real problem.

Sooner or later, you'll be left with the hardcore. Now you can issue whatever consequence their behaviour seems to merit and is in line with your school's behaviour policy, safe in the knowledge that justice has prevailed. The innocent know you are a fair and even-handed judge, and the guilty know they cannot hide behind the collateral damage of their peers.

Next time you're tempted to stoop to collective punishment – and there will be a next time – remember there is an easier, fairer way.

David Didau

Q How do I manage when I've not had much support with classroom behaviour routines?

A You're not alone in this. Many ECTs find themselves thrown into classrooms with the expectation that they'll just *know* how to handle behaviour, even when support is patchy and systems aren't consistent. Especially then. It's frustrating, it's unfair, and it can make you question whether you're cut out for the job. (You are.)

So, what can you do when behaviour routines haven't been clearly taught, reinforced, or backed up by leadership? This is where the Early Career Framework (ECF) can really help. It contains a set of practical, evidence-informed principles that you can use to take control, even when the system feels stacked against you.

Start with the basics: high expectations matter. According to the ECF, setting and maintaining high expectations has a positive impact on both behaviour and learning. That means being clear about what you want, holding that line, and doing so *consistently.* Avoid being strict or shouty; aim for firm, fair, and predictable. That's where routines come in. If you haven't already, choose a small number of routines and teach them explicitly: how to enter the room, how to get your attention, how to move between tasks, how to leave calmly. Keep it simple. Practise them. Narrate them. Model what you want to see.

Praise helps too, but not as a sugar-coating. Use it to reinforce the behaviours you want. 'Thanks for tracking the board, Jayden. That helps everyone focus.' According to the framework, motivation is socially driven. All students want to belong. They want to feel successful. When they see peers being praised for meeting clear expectations, it gives them a reason to follow suit.

You can't rely on memory to track who's doing what, especially when the room is buzzing and your cognitive load is through the roof. That's where having a clipboard comes in. Honestly, a clipboard is one of the most useful, most versatile, and most essential pieces of kit you can invest in. Each morning, print out copies of your class's seating plans and a few reminders about what happened last lesson and anything you need to know (but might forget in the heat of things) about particular students. During the lesson, tick off who's answered questions, put stars next to who said 'I don't know' (and follow up with them), and jot down anything either great or terrible that happens. This isn't about catching students out. It's about clarity, for you and for them. If in the last lesson a student needed regular redirecting, quietly remind them that they can do better today.

When things go wrong – and they will – don't get drawn into debates. Instead, use the ECF's guidance on consistent consequences: keep your tone neutral, offer clear choices, and follow through. Present choices – for example, 'You can choose to get started now and stay in the room, or carry on and we'll have a follow-up conversation at break.' That way, you're calm, consistent, and putting the responsibility where it belongs.

And remember: you don't have to wait for a new term to reset. You can say, 'I've realised I haven't made my expectations clear enough – that's on me. From now on, here's what I expect, and here's how we're going to practise it.' Students won't be shocked; they'll likely feel relieved.

Seek out colleagues whose rooms feel calm and purposeful. Watch how they move, how they speak, what they do when things go wrong. Ask to observe. Use your mentor. Use what the framework teaches: learn from others, reflect on your practice, and keep improving.

Most importantly, be kind to yourself. If you're setting clear rules and routines, reinforcing expectations, and applying fair consequences – as the framework advises – you're doing the right things. It takes time. But if you stick with it, you'll build something that works.

You deserve support. But even in its absence, the principles of the ECF – high expectations, consistent routines, clear modelling – can help you build your own island of calm. Clipboard in hand, routines rehearsed, and expectations firm: you've got this.

David Didau

Q What should I consider when grouping students to support behaviour and engagement?

A Before we talk about any aspect of 'groups', it is important to ask ourselves why we are forming these groups. Groups can be formed for a variety of reasons:

- to work on a specific subject
- geographically laid out in a classroom
- ability groups
- sets within a year group.

If you are going to divide children into groups, ask yourself why. Will it limit children's learning? Does it discriminate against the less able children? How can you be sure you are meeting the needs of every child?

Personally, I very rarely used groups or set group work in a primary context. There are too many things that go wrong, and too many children were left not participating and therefore got very little out of the work. Even if you allocate specific jobs to the children (scribe, researcher, etc.), this takes a lot of time for the children to learn and often descends into the loudest, or most confident, or most able children doing most of the work. Other children become disengaged quickly, and time is wasted.

Setting has pros and cons but is probably best discussed elsewhere. So for this little pearl of wisdom, we shall talk about grouping children in the classroom, whether by ability or randomly, where each child receives the same instruction from the teacher and has similar work to complete (albeit it scaffolded or adapted in some way relevant to the individual needs of the children).

My simple advice for this would be: don't. There are two main reasons why not. First, no matter how you devise the plan, when you have groups of tables in a classroom, there are always several children who have to turn to see the board, and indeed the teacher during instruction. This is uncomfortable and involves a huge amount of chair shuffling and rearranging that wastes time and is disruptive. If there is anything on the whiteboard for support (method of calculation, key words, or modelled answers), then those children will be constantly craning their necks to see the board, then back to their books, then back again.

Second, there are too many opportunities for distraction. When the children have shuffled round and begin their work, when they lift their tiny eyes from the page to ponder or consider, the first thing they see is their friend (usually staring straight back). Children being children, this distracts, and the thought process is lost.

You need to see their faces to assess understanding, and they need to have as little in the way of distraction as possible when you are teaching, so have them in rows, or in a horseshoe. I particularly liked the horseshoe because I would choose particular children to sit at the front when I wanted to work on something specific with them when the class got down to independent work. When children are in rows, you can organise them how you want and to make sure their needs are being met. I cannot tell you the number of times I have been called to a classroom to observe the behaviour of a child, and the answer is that they were distracted by the environment (and by default, where their desk was positioned).

In rows, you can access the whole class systematically to check for misconceptions, or add challenge through questioning and suggestions. When the children are in a group, when you speak they all look up. Rows allow individual feedback discreetly and without distracting others. There are often children who require personalised resources, and using them can often distract on a group table. There are also plenty of children who suffer from low confidence and need assurance, and they are much less likely to ask for help on a group table.

So that is what I have to say on groups in primary schools. I appreciate group work (when done well) can be meaningful and inclusive, but I have to say I have rarely seen it. But sitting in groups, and working in groups are two different things...

Philip Salisbury

Q When is banter not banter?

A In almost 30 years' working with young people in schools, I have never heard a student who was the target of banter say they were just being playfully teased. Banter really gets to me. It annoys me as much as the phrase 'boys will be boys', especially when staff use it to excuse poor behaviour. Adults need to be called out before we start blaming pupils. We set the tone and if we let banter slide we, are part of the problem.

When pupils use banter as an excuse for nasty comments, it must be challenged. Banter is not just a pupil problem. It is a whole-school issue that needs to be addressed openly and consistently. Headteachers should make it clear from the start that there is no place for banter here. This message should be repeated at open evenings and reinforced through regular staff training about language and meaning. If we do not regulate how we talk and what we accept, we risk letting harmful behaviour become normal.

PE teachers have a big responsibility. They need to teach fair play and watch how students speak to each other, especially around sport. Sport often becomes a place where banter is used as a cover for unkindness. Teachers and referees must model decency and stick to school values. When I have stood on the sidelines, I have had to remind my students and sometimes the opposition that we play sport in a principled way. The adult on the pitch is not just there to apply the rules but to set an example of respect and fairness.

There is a difference between teasing that is genuinely playful and teasing that is mean. Nice teasing leaves everyone feeling included and happy. It is based on trust and friendship, and both people know it is light-hearted. The problem is that what is called banter in schools is rarely this kind of teasing. Too often, it is used to mask bullying or to put someone down. If school leaders laugh off banter or treat it as harmless, that is a cultural problem. Young people need to learn the difference between playful teasing and harmful comments, and we need to help them see that.

We should stop giving banter so much attention. If someone says it is only banter, ask them if they were being playfully kind or just unkind. If it is the latter, it needs to stop. Banter should always be checked against the school's core values like kindness, trust, and friendship. If those values are missing, that is a leadership issue. Do not accept banter as harmless. Call it out. In my view, there is no such thing as nice banter. There is only kindness or not.

Richard Clutterbuck

Q As an ECT, how can I tackle misogyny in the classroom?

A One of the most important lessons I've learned as a headteacher, and as someone who still taught, is this: you cannot fix classroom culture in isolation. If the whole-school culture isn't clear, consistent, and lived every day, then asking a new teacher to tackle sexism or misogyny alone is setting them up to fail. Without that foundation, you feel like a lone voice. And lone voices rarely change the room, let alone the school.

This is why leadership matters. Headteachers and senior leaders must shape the positive culture first. They must make it visible, make it routine, and make it stick. When the school's values are more than words on a wall, when they are breathed in every corridor, every conversation, then teachers have the tacit authority to challenge the micro-culture in their classroom. Without that, scripts feel hollow.

In my last school, these three words became our compass: *Trust*, *Kindness*, and *Determination*. They weren't just slogans; they were actions. We encouraged staff and pupils to live them in every moment. We modelled them in assemblies, tutor time, and CPD. We linked them to curriculum content. We called out language in texts. We logged incidents and shared feedback. We put posters everywhere, not because posters change behaviour, but because they remind us what we stand for.

And here's the truth: when pupils and staff start to gently tease you, respectfully, for repeating those values, every time you enter a classroom, however informally, you know you've won. I was gladly teased for saying 'Are you being kind?' so often that it became a running joke. But that joke was the sign that the message had landed. It had become part of the air we breathed – even visiting parents quoted it back at me. And they were thankful.

Even with strong whole-school culture, the classroom is where pupils spend most of their time. It's where micro-cultures form. If staff don't buy in, those micro-cultures drift. That's why scripted responses matter, but only as part of a bigger picture. They give you confidence, they protect the individual who made the comment, and they teach the whole class what is acceptable. But they work best when pupils already know the school's stance.

Scripts that teach, not punish

A good script is short, calm, and consistent. It does three things:

1. **Names the behaviour without naming the pupil.**
   'That comment is sexist. We don't use language like that here.'
2. **Explains why it's wrong.**
   'It puts people down because of their gender, and that's not kind.'
3. **Models the alternative.**
   'If you want to challenge someone's idea, focus on the idea, not who they are.'

Delivered without drama, these responses reinforce the school's values. They say: 'This is how we do things here.' And when every teacher uses them, pupils hear the same message everywhere.

Examples you can use tomorrow

- 'That phrase is disrespectful. Let's keep our language kind and focused on learning.'
- 'We don't use gendered insults here. They're harmful, even if you didn't mean them to be.'
- 'That's not how we talk in this classroom. Try saying it without making it about gender.'

Notice the pattern: firm, fair, and framed as part of a shared standard, not a personal opinion.

The bigger picture

Did it work? Yes. Slowly but surely, pupils start to self-correct and correct each other. They began reporting what they used to ignore. Staff found their voice, confident that they were among the many, not the few. But it starts and finishes with leadership. It starts with values that are lived, not laminated. And it continues in the classroom, where teachers, especially new teachers, need the confidence of scripts and the backing of a culture that says: 'We mean this.'

So, here's my advice: if you're a new teacher, learn the scripts and use them often. But remember, they only work if the school has done the hard work first. And if you're a leader, do that work. Make the values real. Repeat them until they are fired back at you with a smile and respect. Because when they do, you've won.

Richard Clutterbuck

Reflective questions

- How does my classroom setup support focus, inclusion, and positive behaviour?
- When managing conflict, how can I better use restorative approaches to build trust?
- Am I applying behaviour policies in ways that protect students' emotional and physical safety?
- How do my teaching and grouping strategies influence behaviour and engagement in my classroom?

References

Department for Education. (2025) Early years foundation stage (EYFS) statutory framework. GOV.UK. Available at: www.gov.uk/government/publications/early-years-foundation-stage-framework--2

The School Premises (England) Regulations 2012 (SI 2012/1943). Available at: www.legislation.gov.uk/uksi/2012/1943

Education Endowment Foundation (EEF). (2019) *A School's Guide to Implementation: Guidance Report*. Available at: https://educationendowmentfoundation.org.uk/education-evidence/guidance-reports/implementation

Hobson, A. J. and Malderez, A. (2013) 'Judge mentoring and other threats to realizing the potential of school-based mentoring in teacher education.' *International Journal of Mentoring and Coaching in Education*, 2(2), 89–108.

Johnson D. W. and Johnson, R. T. (1989) *Cooperation and competition: Theory and research*. Edina, MN: Interaction Book Company.
Kolb, D. A. (1984) *Experiential Learning: Experience as the Source of Learning and Development*. Prentice Hall.
Montessori, M. (1964) *The Montessori Method*. Schocken Books.
Ofsted. (2023) *Annual report 2022/23: Education, children's services and skills*. GOV.UK. Available at: www.gov.uk/government/publications/ofsted-annual-report-202223-education-childrens-services-and-skills
Sherrington, T. (2019) *Rosenshine's Principles in Action*. John Catt.

5

Children as individuals

Children as individuals also includes children who sit at the margins, whether due to social disadvantage, neurodivergence, trauma, communication needs, or other challenges that affect behaviour. In this chapter, we centre the experiences of these children and provide practical insights into how teachers can respond thoughtfully, ethically, and effectively when behaviour becomes complex.

This chapter brings together the reflections of experienced teachers and leaders who have worked closely with children presenting significant behavioural challenges. Their contributions are not neat or uniform. These are not quick fixes, flowcharts, or scripts designed to work in every classroom. Instead, they are rooted in lived professional experience and an acknowledgement that behaviour is shaped by context, relationships, systems, and adult decision making.

We explore questions that many Early Career Teachers (ECTs) may be asking quietly – but are often afraid to say out loud:

- Is it my fault if my students behave badly?
- Should students be punished for breaking rules?

DOI: 10.4324/9781003592426-5

- How do I balance the needs of one student with the rest of the class?
- What do I do when no strategy seems to work?

Running through this chapter is a deliberate and unresolved tension between different approaches to behaviour. Some contributors foreground agency, boundaries, and the moral importance of consequences. Others emphasise trauma, unmet need, and the necessity of relational, protective, and restorative responses. This is not a contradiction to be smoothed over. It is the reality of classroom life.

ECTs are often presented with false binaries: to *be firm or be kind; punish or understand to hold boundaries or meet needs*. In practice, teachers are required to do all of these things, sometimes within the same lesson, sometimes with the same child. This chapter does not attempt to collapse that complexity into a single ideology. Instead, it asks you to sit with the discomfort, to think critically, and to recognise that professional judgement matters.

In my conversation with **David Didau**, we explore behaviour through the lens of agency, expectations, and consequence, with a particular focus on the story of a student named Ben. While attention deficit hyperactivity disorder (ADHD) was a factor in his exclusion, the discussion moves beyond diagnosis to examine how structure, consistency, and adult authority shape behaviour. David challenges the idea that poor behaviour is simply something that *happens to* teachers, and instead asks ECTs to consider the role of clarity, credibility, and expectation in shaping classroom culture.

This leads into the work of **Jenene Morgan**, an experienced teacher and leader with a deep understanding of how to support children with persistent disruptive or distressed behaviour, without removing them from the classroom. Jenene's contribution is grounded in the belief that children can be held to high expectations *and* supported to meet them. Her work focuses on relationships, routines, and regulation, offering practical strategies that prioritise dignity while maintaining clear boundaries.

Jenene recognises that behaviour is communication, and that exclusion, whether physical or emotional, often compounds the very difficulties schools are trying to resolve. Her message to ECTs is clear: it is possible to manage behaviour well, protect learning, and keep children in the room, but it requires intention, consistency, and emotional literacy.

Krupa Patel brings a trauma-informed safeguarding lens to the chapter, exploring how adverse experiences shape behaviour, regulation, and learning. Drawing on the work of Bruce Perry and Dan Siegel, Krupa explains how trauma affects the developing brain and why some children respond to stress with fight, flight, freeze, or shutdown. Her contribution challenges approaches that prioritise compliance over safety, while also reinforcing the importance of structure, predictability, and adult regulation. Importantly, she situates behaviour firmly within safeguarding, reminding teachers that emotional safety is not optional – it is foundational.

Alongside these contributions, **Phil Beadle** explores disengagement and the often-hidden reasons pupils opt out of learning, as well as the complex question of how teachers can better understand and support white working-class boys, a group too often viewed through the lens of behaviour rather than learning. **Cassie Young** examines the difficult overlap between behaviour and unmet special educational needs, particularly for pupils awaiting assessment or diagnosis, while **Georgina Durrant** challenges common misunderstandings about behaviour in the context of SEND, reframing assumptions around choice, consistency, reward systems, and the quiet behaviours that can mask distress. **Clive Hill** interrogates the concept of aspiration, asking how future-thinking, identity, and belonging shape behaviour, motivation, and self-belief.

Together, these voices do not offer a single answer to behaviour. Instead, they expose its complexity. They show that behaviour is not just about rules, but about relationships, regulation, recognition, and responsibility.

This chapter does not ask you to diagnose children, excuse harm, or abandon boundaries. Nor does it ask you to default to punishment without reflection. It asks you to become a thoughtful, prepared adult in the room, someone who can hold authority without humiliation, compassion without chaos, and consistency without rigidity.

As an ECT, you may find this the hardest and most emotionally demanding part of your role. The child who shouts, swears, shuts down, or lashes out is asking a question – not always in words, but through behaviour:

> *Am I safe? Will you still show up for me? Can you help me learn how to cope?*

This chapter invites you to reframe behaviour not as a battle to be won or a problem to be fixed, but as a conversation between child and adult, one shaped by expectation, context, power, support, and structure. However, the tension remains, and your task is not to eliminate it, but to learn how to navigate it well.

Q How can I engage the disengaged?

A The disengaged child is a problem for the teacher, but perhaps not for obvious reasons. In debating behaviour, many alleged experts reach in the direction of the cosy yet destructive stereotype of the disengaged child disrupting the learning of others. This happens, of course, but far more often the disengaged child is sitting in lessons, present in body but not in spirit, marking out time.

In your early years of teaching, you'll struggle to find a 'why' here. Teachers benefitted from education. Teachers hold its holy flame as being near sacred. Why on earth would anyone reject it?

The disengaged child rejects education for a reason that's probably perfectly valid. Your job is to find it.

In 30 years in a classroom, I've worked with hundreds to thousands of such individuals. And they key is found in the last word of the previous sentence. While there are societal and cultural reasons that cause a lack of engagement with education, there will be reasons specific to the child.

There were various characters in my last school who struggled to engage. Nick was clever but didn't want to be. The most important thing in his life was going fishing with his dad, who didn't believe in education, so neither did he. What do we do in this situation? We try. I found him to be respectful. He was aware that my lessons were viewed well and, initially, he did okay. Ultimately, though, he wasn't bothered.

In these situations, sometimes we have to accept the scoreless draw. We take the smallest wins. We have a strategy. Put them in a chair with an empty chair next to them, and once you've set the task, sit next to the student and support them first. When you've gone to support someone else, they'll go immediately off-task, but keep returning. Take the small victories: the spelling error corrected, the page laid out correctly, the chance to communicate with an adult that cares. Break rules, use humour, give them their own essay title – one they'll find amusing.

Another student in a different class, Alexis, did no work at all. Left to his own devices, he'd place his head on the desk, and while not prone to sleep, he'd drift into a listlessness so total one feared for his mental health. Sometimes you have other priorities than the child who'll not generate results, so, aside from continually informing him that his head should be off the desk, my focus would be on students who would work. Eventually, you find out what the problem is by being human. A while into our 'relationship', I took him outside of the classroom and spoke to him.

'I don't understand, Alexis. You seem to have an awful time in lessons, and they would go less slowly if you engaged a bit. You've got to be here anyway, so why not get what you can out of it?'

'I don't need education.'

It turns out that Alexis was a crypto trader on the side and had already made more money than all his teachers' salaries combined. Crypto has gone up substantially since that time. Maybe Alexis was right.

A further disengaged child, Tom, was profoundly disruptive. His behaviour was disturbed. (There was a reason for this.) I sat him at the front with an empty chair, supported him when I could and was calm when he tried to provoke (this is called 'rage-baiting'). I felt I was failing him, lesson after lesson, until such point that his grandparents, with whom he lived, came to parents' evening.

'I don't know what you've done, Mr. Beadle, but he adores your lessons. He can quote them verbatim.' It turned out that Tom had been subject to profound domestic abuse and was behaving accordingly. The poor child was completely traumatised. 'His behaviour is just checking to see if you're anything like his dad. He says you're the opposite. He finally has an adult that he trusts.'

The point here is that there is a reason for everything. Your job is to find the reason and to temper your behaviour accordingly. Sometimes your response will be to compromise, even to slightly lower your expectations; sometimes your response will be to keep trying for small wins; sometimes your response will be to be the adult that the child needs. You do not win every battle. No one does, and no one ever has. But sometimes, with a disengaged child, if you just keep going, they notice. And when they notice that you care, they start caring.

Phil Beadle

Q How can I support students who have experienced trauma?

A Trauma can have a profound impact on a child's development, and if unresolved, it can shape their relationships and sense of self well into adulthood. As teachers, we may not always know the full story behind a child's behaviour, but we can be a powerful part of their healing journey. This section explores how trauma affects children, offers practical strategies, and underscores the importance of collaboration and self-care in addressing these challenges.

Trauma refers to experiences that overwhelm a child's ability to cope. These experiences may include bereavement, neglect, exploitation, exposure to violence, or verbal, physical, and emotional abuse. The effects are wide-ranging: trauma can disrupt brain development, hinder emotional regulation, impact memory and concentration, and make it difficult to trust others or feel safe. Students affected by trauma may present as anxious, withdrawn, defiant, angry, or overly compliant. Recognising that these behaviours often signal unmet needs – rather than deliberate defiance – is key to providing the right support (Greene, 2014; Perry, 2006).

Be the one to create safety

Your calm presence can become a protective factor in a child's day. Begin with establishing clear, consistent routines that offer predictability and security. Use visuals, provide advance notice of changes, and allow students time to process transitions. These small acts reduce anxiety by helping them feel safe and informed. Greeting students warmly and using a calm, regulated tone can make a significant difference. Every day is a new chance to offer consistency. If an incident occurs, separate the behaviour from the relationship. Repairing trust while maintaining boundaries is crucial. And if you need support after an incident, don't hesitate to ask – your wellbeing matters too.

Thinking points

Where in your classroom can you create a calm area for students to self-regulate when overwhelmed? What regulation strategies or toolkits do you have available – and how can staff support this?

Trauma-informed teaching and learning strategies

Supporting students with trauma means co-creating a learning environment that feels emotionally and physically safe. Here are some core principles and practices to embed into your day-to-day teaching:

- **Flexibility with structure:** High expectations remain important, but adjust tasks, timeframes, and pace when needed. Trauma can affect focus and stamina, so build in flexibility without removing challenge.
- **Sensory support:** Collaborate with the student to identify regulating tools – visuals, movement breaks, noise-cancelling headphones, journalling time, or access to a quiet space. Let support staff know these preferences so they can help embed them consistently.
- **Empathy and curiosity:** Approach behaviours with the mindset 'What might this child be trying to communicate?' This lens allows you to respond with compassion and understanding rather than judgement (van der Kolk, 2014).
- **Celebrating success:** Trauma can make it hard to see progress. Share the wins – however small – with the student and their family. Acknowledging growth reinforces safety, connection, and belonging.

Understanding and managing triggers

Common trauma triggers can include sudden loud noises, certain smells, particular tones of voice, or rapid changes in routine. These are not always obvious, which makes observation key.

- Look for patterns in behaviour that may point to underlying triggers.
- Use direct, non-threatening language, and avoid confrontation where possible.
- Be mindful of your body language – it communicates more than words.
- Ensure behaviour and support plans are shared clearly with all relevant staff.

Above all, be prepared to adjust; sometimes even small changes can make a big difference.

Collaboration and learning

You don't have to figure this out alone. Understanding trauma includes learning about attachment, child development, the physiological effects of stress, and recognising how SEND and medical trauma may influence responses. Meet with your school's SENDCo and pastoral leads to learn more about how trauma manifests and what support is available. These colleagues can help build a holistic picture of the student and co-develop effective responses. Work with safeguarding leads to understand who else is involved in supporting the child – social workers, counsellors, caseworkers. Multi-agency collaboration brings insight, shared expertise, and a stronger safety net. Attend meetings when possible, even if just to listen and learn.

Teaching emotional literacy

Emotional literacy is one of the most powerful things we can offer our students – and ourselves. Understanding how emotions work in the body gives language to feelings and opens doors to regulation. Siegel's (2011) concept of 'flipping your lid' is useful for explaining what happens in the brain when emotions take over. When the amygdala (our emotional centre) overwhelms the prefrontal cortex (our reasoning centre), students may respond with fight, flight, freeze, or complete shutdown. Helping them notice this in themselves, and offering regulation strategies, is a vital step. Practical ways to build emotional literacy include:

- **Breathing routines:** Encourage slow, deep belly breaths throughout the day – not just when things go wrong.
- **Emotional check-ins:** Use charts, journalling, or guided conversations to help students recognise and name their emotions.
- **Conflict role plays:** Model reflective language, perspective taking, and solutions.
- **Movement breaks:** Regular physical activity – even short – can help with emotional processing.

Don't forget: these strategies are just as important for your wellbeing. We model regulation best when we practise it ourselves.

Self-care, realism, and resilience

Supporting students who have experienced trauma is complex. It may not follow a linear path, and some days will feel tougher than others. Progress can be slow, and setbacks may come without warning. It's important to manage your expectations and remind yourself: you are helping to hold space, not carry the full load. Supervision, regular mentoring, and access to quality CPD are essential. Reflect with others, ask for help, and take time to check in with your own feelings. When you are supported, you are more able to offer that sense of safety to your students. And finally, remember that you don't need to have all the answers. Your consistent, caring presence may be the most transformative thing you offer. In a world that may have felt unpredictable or unsafe, you can become the adult who shows up, listens, and believes in them.

Krupa Patel

Q Is it my fault that my students' behaviour is so poor?

A If we believe that children have agency and free will, then it must follow that their behaviour is a choice. If students choose to behave badly in your classroom, it is not your fault. It is, however, your responsibility.

I've seen enough cruelty and cynicism from children to inure me against the belief that being 'good' and 'kind' is in any way natural. Children are capable of being as mean-spirited, spiteful, and selfish as any adult. Human beings generally pursue the course of action that leads to the most reward for the least effort. If behaving well requires less effort and produces greater rewards, they'll behave. But if it seems easier and more socially acceptable to muck about, then they probably will.

When I was a freshly minted teacher, I really struggled with some of my classes. One class I taught was particularly unmanageable, and I would dread their lessons. One morning in briefing, the deputy head in my school asked if anyone needed any support with their classes, and, somewhat naively, I admitted I did. He agreed to visit during my lesson and offer some advice. As usual, the lesson was a shambles, with children wilfully ignoring me and wandering about the room. But when the deputy entered the room, everyone went suddenly silent and slinked, shamefaced, back to their seats. After berating the class, he asked to see me at break-time and went on his way. Needless to say, as soon as the door closed, behaviour immediately began to bubble.

When I met up with the deputy later, he told me he knew what the problem was: He said I hadn't planned my lesson well enough, and therefore the students were bored. This came as a bitter blow as I'd been up till late the night before, valiantly trying to plan a watertight and engaging lesson.

It only came to me much later that this wasn't about my planning. This wasn't the issue. The moment he entered my classroom, students just did what was expected without the need for him to do or say anything. The students behaved differently in his presence because they knew the consequences for misbehaving in front of him. They chose to misbehave for me because they recognised I lacked experience and authority. They knew there were no consequences.

Years later, after acquiring a degree of experience and authority, I was able to have the same effect as that deputy when I walked into a classroom. I didn't have to plan anything. In fact, my classroom was often used by colleagues as a space where they could deposit unruly students so they could get on with the difficult business of teaching.

Some years ago, I taught a boy – let's call him Ben – who had been diagnosed with ADHD. He behaved well in my lessons but was hell on wheels for various other teachers. In particular, his relationship with his French teacher had descended to a running feud, and his attitude towards her was appalling.

Instead of holding him responsible and punishing him, the school decided to confront Ben's outrageous shenanigans by offering him a mentor. And because I got on with him, Ben nominated me as the teacher he most wanted as his guide. After one particularly horrific incident, I confronted him about his behaviour:

Ben: *It's not me, sir, it's my ADHD.*Me: *But how come you don't have ADHD in my lessons?*Ben: *That's cos you're alright, sir.*Ben was exercising a choice. He chose when and where to behave and pay attention. The school's expectation of his behaviour might have been low, but, in the end, he was permanently excluded after committing one atrocity too many. But if the expectation had been for him to follow the rules, we might have done him a far kinder service. At the very least, he'd have had an early lesson about consequences and had more time to settle into a new school.

The belief that children are all little angels corrupted by the adult world is a dangerous but powerful anchor. It prevents us from seeing children as they truly are and makes us feel that if children are not well behaved, it must somehow be our fault. Instead, we need to see children honestly as the complex but immature beings they are – full of soaring beauty and commonplace ugliness. To excuse children's poor behaviour is to deny them any sense of agency and to suggest they are incapable of exercising self-control.

David Didau

Q Should students be punished for breaking school rules?

A Punishment is a bit of a dirty word for many teachers. There often seems to be a presumption that children are naturally good and that any attempt to control or impede their impulses is somehow akin to child abuse. Some schools have banned any form of punishment altogether, and 'behaviourism' is roundly dismissed and has become a touchstone for anyone wanting to argue that children's natural impulses should be understood rather than punished.

B. F. Skinner, the psychologist most closely associated with behaviourism, developed the theory of operant conditioning: if behaviour is rewarded, it is more likely to be repeated, and if it is sanctioned, it's less likely to be repeated. The classic carrot and stick. Skinner described both reinforcements and punishments as being either positive or negative in character. A positive reinforcement is simply the giving of a reward, whereas a negative reinforcement is the removal of a constraint – maybe a student is allowed to leave a lesson early or doesn't have to do their homework. A positive punishment is the active application of a sanction – maybe a good telling-off or a simple glare. A negative punishment is the removal of a privilege – maybe a phone is confiscated, or a student is detained after a lesson.

Surprisingly, despite his reputation, Skinner was against the use of punishment in schools. He believed that even where punishments are consistently applied, they only temporarily suppress undesirable behaviour. If you remember the scene in *Kes* where the smokers are caned, you'll understand his point.

But maybe punishment is a bit more complex than Skinner believed. Research into loss aversion – the asymmetry between the effects of positive reinforcement and negative punishment – show that, on the whole, most people would far rather avoid a loss than make a gain. It seems likely that this effect might also apply to the sorts of merit systems often used in schools. The threat of negative sanctions may be more motivating than the offer of positive rewards.

Punishment appears to effectively promote cooperation in societies with high levels of trust. Members of these societies adhere to norms that encourage both cooperation and the punishment of those who defy cooperative social norms. Punishment seems a less effective deterrent in societies where social norms may be less strongly shared and enforced. The implication is that if students perceive schools as benevolent and trust that teachers have their best interests at heart, the proportionate use of sanctions to support cooperative social norms is likely to be effective.

Maybe if we tried to strip punishment of its more negative connotations, we might feel less squeamish about using it.

David Didau

Q What strategies can I use to support children exhibiting challenging behaviours without asking children to leave the class?

A As an ECT, one of the most important skills you will develop is managing behaviour in the classroom. It's essential to support all children, including those who exhibit challenging behaviours, without resorting to asking them to leave the room. Keeping students in the classroom allows them to remain engaged with their peers, continue learning, and avoid disrupting their connection to the school community. It is important that you are trained appropriately to deal with misbehaviour consistently and fairly for your students to learn to behave appropriately. The *Behaviour in Schools* guidance from the Department for Education (DfE) (February 2024) sets out the expectations for schools and their staff to create and maintain high standards of behaviour. Here are some strategies to support children exhibiting challenging behaviours while ensuring they stay in the classroom.

Building positive relationships

Building strong relationships with your students is fundamental. Take the time to understand each child's background, interests, and needs using all sources available to you – TAs, parents, passports, and education, health, and care plans (EHCPs). Students are more likely to engage positively when they feel respected and understood, and have trusted adults in their lives.

Be consistent in your approach to behaviour management. Ensure that all students know what is expected of them and that there are clear, fair consequences for inappropriate behaviour. Never be afraid to reset if things are not going well or you feel that you have lost consistency due to time constraints or a busy schedule. Take the time to re-establish the classroom rules and explain to the class the reason for the reset.

Use positive reinforcement

Catch students doing the right thing. Praise in public (PIP) and reprimand in private (RIP). How you praise and reprimand students in the classroom can make or break relationships. Every child is different, and what works for one may not work for another. This again highlights the importance of knowing your students. Public praise can be verbal, a round of applause or finger snaps. Non-verbal praise can be a thumbs-up or even just a smile. Using reward systems like stickers, house points, or a 'star of the day/week' helps to encourage positive behaviour. However, it must be meaningful, achievable, and age-appropriate. Positive reinforcement motivates students to repeat good behaviour. It can be a powerful tool to use with your most challenging students.

Create a calm and supportive classroom environment

Establish clear, positive behaviour expectations at the beginning of the year and revisit them regularly. Ensure students understand what behaviours are acceptable and how they contribute to a positive classroom atmosphere. This part is fundamental: just like adults, students need to know why they are doing something and not just be told to 'do it'.

Predictable routines help reduce anxiety and provide structure, especially for children who may struggle with their behaviour. When students know what to expect, they are more likely to stay on track. A quiet space, time-out card, wellbeing room, zones of regulation, or a sensory room are some ways that schools are helping students to regulate their behaviour and wellbeing.

De-escalation techniques

When faced with challenging behaviour:

- Remain calm.
- Do not show frustration or anger.
- Speak slowly, ensuring the student can hear every word.
- Maintain a neutral tone.
- Do not raise your voice.
- Ensure your body language remains open and non-threatening.
- Avoid standing close to the student and looking down on them.
- Speak with empathy.

It helps to give the students choices – for example, 'Would you like to go to the quiet corner or are you ready to start work now?' Offering choices gives children some control of the situation and also gives them a way out of the confrontation without them losing face in front of the class.

Jenene Morgan

Q How do you know when a behaviour issue might actually be an unmet special educational need, and how do you support behaviour for a pupil awaiting assessment or diagnosis?

A There's a phrase I hear too often in schools: 'He's just naughty.' Or its slightly less blunt cousin: 'She knows exactly what she's doing.' Yet when you sit with the child's parents, the SENCo, and perhaps a pastoral lead, the story shifts. Suddenly, you hear about ongoing referrals, concerns raised in multiple settings, and the possibility of an undiagnosed need. This is the uncomfortable middle ground that many teachers, particularly ECTs, find themselves working in: the messy space between behaviour and special educational needs. The question is how you know when behaviour is a signal of something deeper, and what you should do when a pupil is still waiting for the system to catch up with them.

The first principle is to avoid assuming that all behaviour equates to SEND. Behaviour is communication, but it does not automatically mean that the child has an additional need. The SEND Code of Practice (2015) makes this explicit: 'Persistent disruptive or withdrawn behaviours do not necessarily mean that a child or young person has SEN.' Sometimes the behaviour does stem from unmet needs, but at other times it can be explained by poor boundaries, unsettled home circumstances, anxiety, or even just a badly structured lesson that demands too much of the child's working memory. The challenge for teachers is to stay curious rather than rush to label. Asking 'What is this behaviour telling us?' rather than 'What diagnosis fits this behaviour?' is the shift that keeps our practice grounded.

This is where the quality of a school's identification process makes all the difference. A robust system prevents knee-jerk assumptions and gathers a rounded picture before deciding on support. That means classroom observations, ideally by more than one adult across different subjects and contexts. It means listening carefully to the child themselves about what feels difficult, as well as asking parents what they notice at home. It involves looking at assessment data for patterns in literacy, language, attention, or working memory, and it means scrutinising the child's work to see whether difficulties are conceptual misunderstandings or barriers linked to processing and executive functioning. This is often referred to as 'slow noticing': holding back from hasty conclusions long enough to spot the consistent patterns underneath. It is not glamorous, but it is what stops us from either missing a genuine need or prematurely adding a child to the SEN register when the issue lies elsewhere. Most importantly, this process must be led collaboratively. The SENCo cannot work in isolation, and teachers cannot outsource all responsibility to 'the SEN department'. Identification is a collective effort, and the quality of teaching and curriculum access remains the first and most important intervention.

That said, many teachers face the real frustration of supporting pupils who are 'in the system' but stuck waiting for assessment or diagnosis. In practice, waiting lists can be years long, and families are often worn down by the sheer effort of referrals and paperwork. In this limbo, teachers must act. The worst approach is to do nothing and say, 'We'll wait and see.' You don't need a diagnosis to make a classroom accessible. If a child is visibly struggling with concentration, you can adapt your language, reduce task size, use visuals, and break the work into manageable chunks. If they cannot cope with unstructured group work, you can give them a defined role or scaffolded steps. If the noise level is overwhelming, you can create a quieter workspace.

Small adjustments send a powerful message that the child's needs are being taken seriously even before the paperwork catches up.

This is not to say that expectations should be abandoned. Supporting a potential need does not mean lowering the bar. Boundaries remain important, but the route to reaching them may look different. A pupil may still be expected to finish their work, but the way the task is structured or the time frame provided might be altered. Calm consistency, rather than either harsh sanction or unstructured indulgence, is what helps pupils thrive in this uncertain period.

Crucially, teachers are not expected to carry the burden alone. Collaboration is key. The SENCo should always be the first point of reference, but there is much to learn from colleagues who have taught the child previously, from the designated safeguarding lead (DSL) if safeguarding factors are in play, from families who may share valuable insights, and from support staff who often notice the micro-interactions that classroom teachers miss. Sometimes the breakthrough lies in something apparently small but profoundly significant: the child who had undetected glue ear for three years and never properly heard phonics teaching, or the child masking anxiety until it erupts as refusal. Gathering these perspectives makes for a more nuanced and compassionate response.

The stakes are high. If we conflate SEND and behaviour without care, we risk both over-identifying and under-identifying children. In one direction, every child with challenging behaviour ends up labelled, which dilutes the integrity of the SEN register. In the other direction, children with genuine needs are dismissed as 'just naughty' and left unsupported until crisis point. Neither outcome serves inclusion, and neither helps pupils flourish.

The alternative is to use behaviour as data, to stay curious and notice carefully, to adapt teaching even without a label, and to build a collaborative evidence base that supports accurate identification later. This is not about becoming an amateur diagnostician. It is about being the kind of teacher who notices, who adapts, and who keeps boundaries steady while understanding that behaviour is rarely as simple as it first appears. As Dylan Wiliam reminds us, teachers don't need to improve because they are not good enough; they need to improve because they can be even better. Nowhere is that more true than in navigating the intersection of behaviour and unmet need.

Cassie Young

Q What are some common misunderstandings teachers have about behaviour and SEND, and how can we reframe them?

A Understanding behaviour in the context of pupils with SEND can sometimes be complicated. Behaviour is such a complex and emotive subject that it's easy for misunderstandings to occur. These misunderstandings aren't intentional, but I would stress that they can still have a profound impact on how children and young people are supported, and we therefore need to reflect on them. I often think by reframing these misunderstandings, we can create classrooms that feel more inclusive, compassionate, and effective. Our ultimate goal!

A common misconception is that behaviour is always a choice. I've been there, and I know that when a pupil shouts out, refuses to follow instructions, or walks out of class, it can feel like deliberate defiance. Yet taking a step back and reflecting, it's clear that for many children with SEND, behaviour is a form of communication rather than a conscious decision. An autistic child, for example, might leave the classroom because the noise is overwhelming. Or another child may struggle to sit still not because they want to disrupt but because they may need movement to remain regulated.

Reframing this means shifting our perspective. This could be changing the question we have of 'Why won't they behave?' to instead thinking 'What are they trying to tell me?' That small change in mindset opens the door to understanding their needs.

Another misunderstanding is that consistency means treating everyone the same. As an Newly Qualified Teacher (NQT), I remember being encouraged to be consistent in my actions with regard to behaviour. And being told that consistency was the key to good behaviour in the classroom. But I think we forget that consistency does not mean identical treatment. And inclusion isn't about treating everyone the same. For pupils with SEND, fairness and equity often means flexibility. A child with dyslexia, for example, may need instructions broken down into smaller steps or written text chunked. A child with sensory processing difficulties may need to wear headphones during assemblies. Reframing consistency means recognising that equity is about giving each child what they need to succeed, not insisting on one-size-fits-all rules to make it 'fair'.

Traditional behaviour/reward systems such as stickers, verbal warnings, points, or detentions are often assumed to work for everyone. While they may be effective for many pupils, they don't always work for children with SEND. A child with anxiety may find the threat of a sanction paralysing rather than motivating. A child with processing difficulties may not connect the consequence with the behaviour if too much time has passed. Reframing this means thinking creatively. I'm definitely not suggesting abandoning boundaries, but instead working out ways to ensure equity, inclusion, and flexibility in tailoring approaches to the individual child or young person. It's also often easy to end up focusing our attention on the more obvious, disruptive behaviours in the classroom, but we mustn't forget that the other extreme – quiet behaviour – can also (but not always) signal that a child or young person could be struggling. Silence can feel reassuring to us as teachers, yet for some pupils with SEND, it may be masking distress rather than reflecting engagement. A child with situational (selective) mutism may be unable to speak in class, and their quietness is certainly not compliance, but anxiety. Similarly, a child who is masking may appear calm and settled, while inside they are exhausted and overwhelmed. It's so important to recognise that behaviour isn't only about what we see on the surface; it's about checking in with the child's emotional state and remembering that calmness doesn't always equal comfort.

Finally, many teachers feel they must manage behaviour alone, that reaching out shows weakness, when, in fact, the opposite is true – it shows you value collaboration. Behaviour often requires a team approach, especially if the child has SEND: SENDCos, teaching assistants, healthcare professionals who are supporting, and (most importantly) families all have valuable insights. Asking for support is part of professional practice and duty, not a sign of failure. Ultimately, reframing behaviour in the context of SEND is about empathy and curiosity. It's about moving from 'How do I stop this behaviour?' to 'How do I understand and support this child?' That shift can genuinely transform classrooms into places where pupils with SEND can thrive, and teachers feel empowered rather than overwhelmed.

Georgina Durrant

Q What can I do to support white working-class boys?

A Nearly 20 years ago, I was much delighted (and even a tad honoured) to be invited to speak to the headteachers in the London borough in which I grew up: Bromley. I was further delighted to learn that the speech was to be on one of my specialisms and my abiding passion – white working-class children. The glee didn't last to the end of the sentence on the invitation. The thing I was to talk about was white working-class boys and their behaviour problems.

Which leads us to the root of the issue…

All the time we view one of the largest sub-groups of our school population through the lens of behaviour, we fail to see them through the lens of learning.

You'll hear this often because it is true: white boys on free school meals are the lowest-attaining socio-economic group in English education. The reasons for this are multifarious, complex, and interlinked, but one of them is a kind of reverse Pygmalion effect.[1] We don't actually expect them to achieve, and they suss this out about us. What a teacher believes seeps out of every pore of their being. You may think you're a skilled actor and can successfully mask your suppositions, your biases, your unconscious prejudice, but here's the news: generally speaking, you can't.

The first job of any teacher is one of belief. You must believe that it is important to believe[2] the seemingly naïve mantra that 'any child can achieve any outcome'. Get your heart right, and your head and body will follow.

More recently, but, again, years ago, I was invited by a school in my home borough to speak about the barriers affecting the achievement of these boys. I agreed to do so but asked to meet a group of the boys first to see what the issues were that they faced and what it was about specific teachers that helped them to achieve. One student came up with an answer that might be used to inform every interaction you have with a student from this socio-economic group. When asked what behaviours characterised teachers who get the best out of them, he replied, 'They approve of you.'

Carry the following three simple words in your heart. Approve of them.

You are dealing with young people who have a very specific (and, indeed, historic) culture, and it is your job to reach out to that culture,

1 This is the idea that teacher expectations are a self-fulfilling prophecy. It was originated by psychologists Robert Rosenthal and Leonore Jackson in a book of the same name. It's well worth a look.

2 Look at the wording here. It is deliberate. What am I trying to say? What fine distinction is being made?

to not give them any sense that you think you are in any way better than them. In that culture, if the dads are still present, they are often revered. In that culture, the family is everything. Once you have passed the early stages of winning their trust, ask them, casually, how the family is. Find out what the parents do. If they're working, pay explicit respect to that work. If you have to have a chat with them outside of the class, try the following phrasing: 'Just imagine that I was not just a teacher but was actually a real, live human being and that I care about you…' Approve of them.

And also, while there's an element of the job that means all teachers have to pay lip service to the claims of education, don't believe for one moment that achievement in academic subjects is all that school cracks it up to be or that school fulfils that many of the false promises education makes about itself to such children. They can see through them. It may be that the child who doesn't really care about their GCSEs will have a perfectly happy and very successful life. Whisper it, but GCSEs aren't actually that important. When was the last time you were asked about yours? I come from a very large, extended white working-class family. I'm one of only a very few with any academic qualifications, and I'm the only one who's got no money.

Phil Beadle

Q What has aspiration got to do with behaviour?

Walking the tightrope: Balancing passion and pragmatism in education

A In the realm of education, teachers often find themselves walking a tightrope, delicately balancing the ideal of nurturing a love for their subject with the pragmatic need for students to study for future employment. This challenge becomes particularly evident during key transition moments, such as when students in their final year of pre-16 education visit colleges and return with the attitude of 'I only need Maths and English' (not the message from good colleges!). This mindset, driven by both innate and extrinsic motivations, can create tension in the classroom, as teachers strive to instil a passion for learning while recognising the reality of job market demands.

The term 'aspiration' frequently appears in school mission statements and ethos, often implying that success is defined by high grades, prestigious degrees, and conventional career paths. This narrow view can lead to detrimental comparisons among students, as seen when one student tells another they 'failed' a subject despite achieving a Grade 3. It's crucial for educators to recognise the impact of language and expectations on students' self-perceptions and motivations. We must shift our focus from traditional notions of success to a more inclusive understanding that celebrates individual progress and diverse career paths.

As educators, we have a responsibility to use language that fosters a positive learning environment. By reframing how we discuss grades and career aspirations, we can help students understand that there are multiple paths to success. Celebrating achievements, regardless of their scale, reinforces the idea that progress is valuable. For example, acknowledging a 'strong Level 1 pass' can motivate students to strive for further improvement, rather than labelling them as failures.

This approach is particularly important in addressing biases that may arise from our own backgrounds. Teachers often inadvertently project middle-class aspirations on to students from diverse economic backgrounds. It is essential to cultivate a culture where every student feels empowered to pursue their ambitions, whether that means becoming a tradesperson, being an entrepreneur, or pursuing higher education.

The role of the careers lead is critical in guiding students toward informed decisions about their futures. Many students have aspirations that may not align with traditional academic routes, yet they possess the potential to thrive in vocational fields. For instance, students interested in hairdressing or construction may not be aware of the entrepreneurial opportunities within these industries. By exposing students to a broad range of possibilities and supporting them in developing their skills, we can help them recognise their potential as wealth generators and job creators in their communities.

Embedding career education within the pastoral framework of schools can significantly impact students' self-efficacy and motivation. It's essential to foster meaningful conversations about futures where students can envision themselves succeeding, thus reinforcing their agency in shaping their career paths.

To nurture intrinsic motivation, we must help students see the value of their education in a broader context. Education is not just a means to an end but a lifelong journey that equips them with the skills and knowledge necessary for various career pathways. By fostering a growth mindset, we encourage students to view challenges as opportunities for learning, rather than insurmountable obstacles.

For students who may feel disengaged or are at risk of exclusion, it is vital to create a sense of belonging and purpose. This can be achieved by helping them identify their strengths and interests, and guiding them toward careers that align with their passions. When students feel successful, they are more likely to engage with their education and pursue their aspirations with enthusiasm.

The challenge remains: how do we make education enjoyable while maintaining high expectations? The answer lies in recognising that enjoyment is closely tied to success. When students feel successful in their studies, they are more likely to engage with the material and develop a genuine interest in the subject matter. This connection can be reinforced by providing clear pathways for students to achieve their goals, whether through vocational training, apprenticeships, or traditional academic routes.

Moreover, it is essential for educators to communicate effectively with students, ensuring they understand the grading system and the significance of their achievements. By eliminating the stigma associated with lower grades and focusing on progress and potential, we can create a healthier culture of motivation and personal success.

The tightrope of education requires teachers to balance fostering a love of their subject with the pragmatic need for students to prepare for future employment. By embracing a holistic approach to career education, using inclusive language, and cultivating intrinsic motivation, we can empower students to pursue their passions while also understanding the practical implications of their education. Ultimately, our goal should be to help every student recognise their potential and navigate their own unique pathways to success, ensuring they feel valued and capable in their educational journey.

Clive Hill

Reflective questions

- When behaviour becomes challenging, where do I instinctively position myself – towards consequences and boundaries or towards understanding and support – and why?
- How do I decide when to hold firm and when to be flexible? What guides my judgement in the moment?
- What messages does my classroom send about safety, power, and belonging, especially to children who struggle most?
- How do my responses to behaviour affect learning over time, for both the individual child and the wider group?
- Where might aspects of my teaching, routines, or classroom structure be contributing to the behaviour I see?
- How confident am I in using trauma-informed approaches without lowering expectations or avoiding difficult conversations?
- When behaviour feels complex or overwhelming, who do I seek support from, and do I do so early enough?
- In moments of difficulty, what kind of adult do I want my students to experience me as, and how close am I to that in practice?

References

Department for Education (DfE). (2024) *Behaviour in Schools: Advice for headteachers and school staff.* Available at: https://assets.publishing.service.gov.uk/media/65ce3721e1bdec001a3221fe/Behaviour_in_schools_-_advice_for_headteachers_and_school_staff_Feb_2024.pdf

Department for Education & Department of Health. (2015) SEND code of practice: 0 to 25 years (para. 6.21). GOV.UK. Available at: www.gov.uk/government/publications/send-code-of-practice-0-to-25

Greene, R. W. (2014) *The Explosive Child: A New Approach for Understanding and Parenting Easily Frustrated, Chronically Inflexible Children* (5th ed.). HarperCollins.

Perry, B. D. (2006) *The Boy Who Was Raised as a Dog: And Other Stories from a Child Psychiatrist's Notebook*. Basic Books.

Rosenthale, R. and Jacobson, L. (1968) *Pygmalion in the Classroom: Teacher Expectation and Pupils' Intellectual Development*. Holt, Rinehart and Winston.

Siegel, D. J. and Bryson, T. P. (2011) *The Whole-Brain Child: 12 Revolutionary Strategies to Nurture Your Child's Developing Mind*. Delacorte Press.

Van der Kolk, B. A. (2014) *The Body Keeps the Score: Brain, Mind, and Body in the Healing of Trauma*. Penguin Books.

Wiliam, D. (2018) *Creating the Schools Our Children Need: Why What We're Doing Now Won't Help Much (and What We Can Do Instead)*. Learning Sciences International.

6

Children and their parents/carers

When we talk about behaviour in schools, the focus is often on children themselves, classrooms, or the strategies that teachers use. Yet behaviour never exists in isolation: it is shaped by systems, culture, and the web of relationships that extend beyond the school gates. Among these, carers play a significant and powerful role. Every teacher, irrespective of whether they are an Early Career Teacher (ECT) or an experienced leader, will know or find out that behaviour can't be fully understood or supported without acknowledging and recognising parents/carers as key people within this process.

As **Dr Dan Owen** acknowledges, parents/carers do not encounter behaviour through policy documents or websites first; they experience it through their children, through conversations in the community, and through the tone and culture of the school. They find out on social media websites, through gossip around the area, or, as I recently experienced when passing my local school, that child vaping outside school. What parents/carers believe about behaviour in a school becomes the narrative in which they view staff and teaching, and they place a value on whether their child will be safe within that school environment. These beliefs and values may match what is happening

DOI: 10.4324/9781003592426-6

in the classroom and school community or they can diverge from the reality. Irrespective, these perceptions matter.

This chapter explores how schools and teachers can understand and shape those narratives, begin to build strong partnerships with parents/carers, and handle the most challenging conversations with both clarity and empathy. The voices of different contributors highlight how carers find out about behaviour in schools, how ECTs can establish strong relationships early, and how difficult conversations can be approached without becoming adversarial.

For new teachers, this is not an optional extra or a 'nice to have'. The Early Career Framework emphasises the importance of working with parents and carers, of understanding the wider context of pupils' lives, and of communicating effectively with stakeholders. By examining carer engagement in relation to behaviour, this chapter invites you to broaden your perspective and to see every interaction as another way of building a positive, inclusive school culture.

In his second contribution, **Dr Dan Owen** considers a practical ECT concern: how to talk to carers about behaviour without the conversation becoming negative or adversarial. His insights stress the importance of careful language, clear theory of action, and the role of every meeting as an opportunity to build partnership.

Phillip Salisbury builds on this theme with practical advice on how ECTs can establish positive relationships with parents early. He highlights the importance of first impressions: greeting children at the door, creating purposeful classrooms, and making early positive phone calls home. These small but deliberate acts help parents see that their child is valued, making later conversations about behaviour or learning more constructive. He also offers guidance on handling sensitive discussions, particularly around SEND, and stresses the importance of seeking support from mentors, SENDCos, and senior leaders.

Richard Clutterbuck reminds us that behaviour does not sit only within classrooms or policies but within the wider culture and community around a school. Parents/carers actively construct and share narratives based on what they see, hear, and experience, whether that's a post on social media, a conversation in the playground, or an incident witnessed outside the gates. Schools cannot control every story, but they can influence perceptions by ensuring consistency between stated values and lived experiences, by communicating clearly and honestly, and by building trust over time. His contribution challenges ECTs to think about how they manage not only behaviour itself but also the *story of behaviour* that parents and carers come to believe.

Georgina Durrant makes the case that genuine partnership with parents and carers is central to supporting the behaviour of pupils with SEND. She argues that listening comes first, because families of children with SEND have often felt unheard, and that schools should share observations rather than judgements, keep communication regular and positive, and align strategies between home and school wherever possible. Her core message is that working with families isn't about passing responsibility over to them; it's about recognising everyone is on the same team, and that when home and school collaborate, behaviour becomes less about conflict and more about connection and belonging.

Hannah Hall draws on her extensive experience to offer two contributions that speak directly to the moments many ECTs quietly dread. In her first contribution, she addresses the fear of saying the wrong thing in conversations with parents and carers, offering honest reflections and practical language for everything from positive phone calls to difficult behaviour discussions and high-stakes parents' evenings. Her advice bridges the gap between primary and secondary contexts, acknowledging that the rhythms of parent communication differ significantly between these phases. In her second contribution, she explores what to do when families don't engage at all, and challenges the assumption that silence is synonymous with disinterest.

Q How do carers find out about behaviour in school?

A 'Carer engagement is paramount to pupils' behaviour in schools.' The axiom that carer engagement is important is so easily said and believed, and yet too rarely explored. What does it mean for a carer to 'engage' and what is it they are engaging with?

The first carer exposure to the behaviour norms and expectations is not likely to be the behaviour policy or the school website. It's likely to be what a carer hears from other carers or the experience of older siblings. It's worth asking ourselves: what sort of reputation does a school have in terms of behaviour? This information is useful to schools. Carers entrust their children to us each day. We want them to have the confidence that their child is in an orderly and calm environment where they are safe and can develop and thrive.

Regardless of the reality in school, the different experiences and perspectives held by carers and shared among a community form vicarious narrative experiences. These become the mental models that communities hold about how pupils behave in school and what the norms and expectations are. Gaining a clear view of these narratives is an essential starting point in engaging carers. Sometimes communities have a view of behaviour in a school that doesn't match the way school staff see behaviour. The reality of behaviour in classrooms and around school isn't what drives carer engagement – remember that communities piece their views together from what they hear from others, including their children.

Schools are more successful in engaging carers if they proactively listen and think carefully about how all communications build into the bigger picture of carer engagement. For example, does the behaviour policy read like a legalistic, criminal-justice-style diatribe, or does it positively outline how everyone will work together to ensure behaviour is good? How do staff speak to carers, and what is the level of intentionality in those staff–carer discussions? How do newsletters build the narrative, and do carers even read them?

At the heart of this is a foundation of high expectations. Sometimes pupils' behaviour in schools can be poor. Sometimes poor behaviour is widespread. Sometimes it's a small number of pupils whose behaviour is difficult, public, defiant, or disruptive. Even when weak behaviour is happening only in 'pockets', there is very little that grinds school staff down more. The outcome is clear: pupils learn less and are interrupted more, teachers become frustrated, and staff fall into negative cycles of response.

Where behaviour is weak, pupils often don't feel safe. This doesn't usually mean chaos, but rather that the flow of learning is frequently interrupted, adults shout, or unstructured times become rowdy and intimidating. Carers hear about this from their children, and it feeds into the narrative picture. Building a positive carer narrative around high expectations and safety is therefore not an optional extra – it is foundational to how carers come to 'know' a school.

Dr Dan Owen

Q How can I involve parents and carers in supporting safeguarding and positive behaviour at school?

A When I joined my second school as a senior deputy head, I assumed I'd earned the right to hit the ground running. I'd built strong relationships and a solid reputation over nine years at my previous school. I thought those same habits and levels of respect would naturally carry over into this new setting.

But I quickly discovered that even experience doesn't replace consistency – and that respect, routines, and rapport aren't portable. I hadn't laid the foundations with this new class, and it showed. Because I hadn't been there from day one, I had to work harder to establish the expectations and routines I wanted.

At the same time, we welcomed a newly qualified geography teacher to the school. I spent time observing her lessons and was amazed. Her classroom was calm, purposeful, and respectful. Her students, across the full spectrum of needs and behaviours, were deeply engaged.

When I asked her what her secret was, her answer floored me: during the first term, from September to December, she called the parents of every child she taught at least once, more often two to three times. Not because something had gone wrong, but because she wanted to share something positive.

Those consistent conversations built trust with parents, which then transferred into trust and cooperation in the classroom. She was building culture at both ends, home and school, and it worked. I took her lead and started doing the same. Before long, I saw the impact. Relationships grew stronger, routines became embedded, and a sense of mutual respect developed quickly.

That experience reshaped how I see the role of families in both safeguarding and behaviour. They're not just part of the support network – they're co-creators of school culture.

My approach to behaviour also changed dramatically over time. I used to dread calling home about a pupil's behaviour. It felt like delivering bad news, and I often avoided it longer than I should have, but once I started building relationships through positive contact, everything shifted. A quick call home to say 'Your child really impressed me today' not only made a parent's day, but it also laid the groundwork for support when tougher conversations were needed. Parents became more invested. They weren't just reacting to problems, they were joining in solutions, and I stopped seeing myself as the sole enforcer of expectations.

Another game changer? I started asking a member of SLT (senior leadership team) to visit my classroom daily, not because there was an issue, but to reinforce visibility, consistency, and shared responsibility. It sent a message to pupils that behaviour expectations weren't just 'mine' – they were part of the whole school ethos. It also gave me a sounding board and moral support in real time, which made a real difference.

Safeguarding: Shared culture, shared responsibility

One of the most important shifts in my thinking came when I realised that safeguarding isn't just a school responsibility; it's a shared culture that must include parents and carers. In schools, we often focus on the formal aspects: training, reporting procedures, and protocols. These are essential, but they're only part of the picture. The real power comes when families understand, trust, and feel part of that safeguarding culture.

This doesn't happen through one-off policies or information evenings. It happens through ongoing micro-conversations – quick chats at pick-up, friendly reminders about online safety, or explaining the importance of reporting concern – and macro-conversations – inviting families to take part in shaping policies, attending safeguarding workshops, or contributing to the school's overall wellbeing strategy.

When we demystify safeguarding and show that it's not just something 'we do' but something 'we share', families are more likely to reach out when they see a problem, and more likely to partner with us before issues escalate.

Trust builds early and often. And when it's there, safeguarding becomes proactive, not just reactive.

Five takeaways for new teachers

1. **Call early, call often, and keep it positive:** Establish communication with parents before problems arise. A positive phone call in week one builds trust you can rely on later.
2. **Treat safeguarding as a shared culture:** Make safeguarding part of both micro (daily) and macro (strategic) conversations with families. Trust and transparency matter more than jargon or policy.

3. **Ask SLT to be present, even when things are fine:** Regular visits from SLT help normalise support and show that behaviour culture is a shared priority, not just a crisis-response measure.
4. **Be clear and consistent with expectations:** Use plain, accessible language when sharing routines or behaviour policies with parents. When they understand the 'why', they're more likely to reinforce it at home.
5. **See families as co-creators, not just recipients:** Involve parents in understanding your classroom and school culture. Invite their input, listen deeply, and treat them as partners in every sense.

If I could give my younger self one piece of advice, it would be this: you don't have to do it alone. Invite parents into the conversation at least, not just when you have to, but because it builds something better for everyone.

Richard Clutterbuck

Q How can ECTs build strong relationships with parents, and why does this matter for behaviour and learning?

A Establishing good relationships with parents is essential for many reasons, and children benefit more when there is a strong relationship and good communication between the two.

Working with parents starts on the first day the child attends school. Setting high expectations is essential. When I speak to ECTs about the first day in the class, one of the things I insist upon is that they are at the door to greet the children and a create a positive atmosphere. Being organised, having a purposeful classroom, giving children your attention all demonstrates to the children that they matter and that the teacher cares for them. Another thing I insist upon is that they have things ready for the children to do from the second they enter the classroom. There is nothing worse for a child than to enter a room and have to find something to do in a disorganised and rowdy classroom. Selecting activities that are appropriate for the children (and as the year goes on, these will become more individualised) to do as soon as they enter the classroom sets an expectation that learning matters.

The reason I mention these things in relation to parents is that it will instil in the child a belief that you care for them, and this is essential. If the child returns home happy and believes you care, parents are much more relaxed, and future communication with them is easier. To set the tone for your relationship with parents, another thing we do is ensure that within the first week of school our teachers have spoken to every single parent at least once about something positive. It doesn't have to be a long conversation, and it must be sincere, but a ten-second conversation can go a long way to getting parents on side. Something along the lines of 'He's had a great day today, he's worked really hard' or 'She was fantastic today, did really well in her maths' can transform the way a child thinks about school and indicates to the parent that you value their child. If you don't see the parents of a child, then we ask our ECTs to call home and just quickly mention what a good day that child has had.

In every year group, there are some children whose parents you will need to talk to about something negative. These conversations are much easier if you've already had four or five conversations with them about something good their child has done. Parents are much likelier to accept criticism or receive negative reports about behaviour if they think you care about their child and you know them. Those first few interactions with parents must be positive and must show that you value their child.

When it comes to dealing with parents over a behaviour matter or a learning matter, as an ECT it is really important that you discuss it with a member of SLT or your mentor. It is also a good idea to find out who the previous teacher was and see if there were similar issues and how they were dealt with. There may also be safeguarding issues that you are unaware of, so before you embark on any conversation with parents, it is a good idea to speak to senior people at the school first.

There are two types of conversation you are likely to have with parents, and I'll deal with these separately.

The first one is behaviour. In all conversations with parents, context matters, and you will have to adapt the conversation according to the relationship you have with the parent. Some parents are easier to talk to than others, and there are various reasons for this; however, whatever the circumstances, these tips will help:

- Don't have the conversation in front of other parents.
- Put the behaviour in context and explain clearly what's happened.
- Explain to the parents what the impact of that behaviour was.
- Tell the parent how you've resolved it, and explain to them that you are letting them know.
- Don't be judgemental or disapproving as this often comes across as patronising; remember, it is the behaviour you're talking about.
- End the conversation positively and remind the child and the parent of all the good things that the child has done this year. I finish with something like 'So tomorrow let's start again and make sure this doesn't happen again'.

If the behaviour continues, then you will need to escalate this so talk to a member of SLT and/or your mentor. Various strategies can be used, but schools will differ on how they deploy them. Individual approaches like behaviour charts can work if done effectively, but if this behaviour is continuing, you will need to familiarise yourself with the school policy.

The second type of conversations are those we might have regarding special needs. Again, the context is key, and it is essential that you've established a good relationship with the parents. Before any conversation with them takes place, you should have discussed your concerns with your mentor and the SENDCo. It is important to identify and be clear what the actual problem is and how this is manifesting in class. Statements like 'She doesn't listen' or 'I've told him, but he wasn't concentrating' are not helpful. If necessary, start to take notes and try to observe what the child is doing. If you have a TA, it is sometimes useful to ask them to observe the child and note what they're doing. Try to be clear with what the actual problem is. The more information you can give to the SENDCo the better, and you should try some strategies yourself to see if you can help the child to learn more effectively.

When it comes to discussing a suspected SEND need, schools differ on who will have that conversation. In my school, the conversation is held with the SENDCo. These conversations are often upsetting for parents and should be handled sensitively. It is important to discuss the facts and not allow emotion or speculation to be a part of the conversation. Some parents will think this is the end of the world for their child; it is important that you reassure them, and you have a clear plan for how you will help the child. A review date should be set when you can meet the parents again and update them on the progress the child is making.

Philip Salisbury

Q As a new teacher, how do I talk with carers about behaviour without the conversation becoming negative or adversarial?

A Thinking about times when school staff need to address carers about behaviour, it is important to explore what carers are actually engaging with. They are engaging with a member of staff who is representing the school. Every discussion is an opportunity to build positive narratives about behaviour. For this reason, strong mental models and a clear theory of action are vital.

Let's imagine two pupils have been deliberately tapping on their desks to undermine a lesson. If this has led to a meeting with carers, then warnings and sanctions have already failed. The key question becomes: How can the carer help us to change the pupils' behaviour, and how might we facilitate that?

Carers sometimes arrive at school expecting to be 'told off'. Diane Reay's research in the 1990s showed that mothers' relationships with schools were highly moderated by social class and their own experiences of education. These histories matter. If we hold a mental model that behaviour does not define the child and that a child's behaviour does not define the carer's effectiveness, then we open space for partnership. The aim is not to win a battle but to build collaboration.

Language is crucial. Saying 'Sam is a defiant student' feels very different to a carer compared with 'Sam seems to be struggling to make the right choices recently. He can sometimes come across as defiant.' One defines the child; the other describes behaviour. Similarly, 'If this continues, we will have to consider exclusion' feels more threatening than 'We need to give Sam a chance to think about how he wants to behave and avoid further sanctions'. These small differences signal whether the meeting feels adversarial or supportive.

A theory of action helps here: What do I want this meeting to achieve, and how will my actions lead us there? If our actions don't align with the outcome – improving behaviour – we risk wasting energy or even damaging the relationship. For ECTs, this means going into any carer conversation with clarity: What message do I want to land, what tone will best achieve it, and how will the carer feel when they leave the meeting?

Above all, remember that carers' views of school behaviour are often second-hand or historical. They may already carry negative assumptions. As a new teacher, there is an opportunity to be deliberate. Choose language carefully, build rapport, and keep the focus on partnership. When behaviour is framed around shared high expectations and positive futures, carers are more likely to join you in supporting change.

Dr Dan Owen

Q What if I say the wrong thing?

A If there's one truth I've learned over 25 years in schools, it's this: relationships with parents and carers make or break your work as a teacher. Pupils clock straight away whether school and home are pulling in the same direction. When those relationships are strong, behaviour and learning are far more settled. When they're strained, teaching becomes much harder than it needs to be.

As an ECT, you've probably been overloaded with input on lesson planning, assessment, and classroom management. But if you're honest, how much time has anyone spent training you on how to have a constructive conversation with a parent? For most of us, it has been assumed that, because we're adults and professionals, we'll 'just know what to say'. Let me reassure you: many teachers find the first few conversations with families far more daunting than standing in front of a full class.

Primary and secondary: Different worlds

Your context matters.

In primary schools, families see you every day at the classroom door. They'll catch you on the playground or at pick-up and expect quick updates. That immediacy can help you build rapport naturally, but it also means you can feel 'on duty' from 8.30am to 3.30pm. Boundaries are essential.

In secondary schools, the rhythm is very different. Families rarely see you face-to-face. Contact tends to be more formal – an email, a phone call, or a five-minute slot at parents' evening. The risk is that parents only hear from you when something has gone wrong. You'll need to be much more intentional about building those relationships early, rather than waiting for a crisis to force the conversation. When parents only hear from you when something has gone wrong, you've already put yourself on the back foot.

Why it matters

Strong home–school partnerships aren't a 'nice to have' – they're core business. They:

- **Give pupils consistency:** If home and school are aligned, routines and expectations stick.
- **Build trust:** Parents are more likely to support you if they believe you understand and value their child.
- **Prevent escalation:** A quick, positive phone call can stop a minor niggle becoming a formal complaint.
- **Create belonging:** Families who feel respected and welcomed pass that feeling of safety on to their children.

We are not really taught how to do this. You've probably had more training on phonics, adaptive teaching, or assessment grids than on what to say in a difficult phone call. Yet one clumsy conversation can undo months of graft in the classroom. Add to that the fact that many of us (including parents) are more comfortable with messaging apps or voice notes than with picking up the phone, it's no wonder so many ECTs can sometimes dread calling home.

But here's the good news: with some practice, a few scripts, and a proactive mindset, you can turn those calls and meetings into one of your greatest strengths.

Some families are used to hearing bad news from school. Flip that script by making recognition part of your weekly rhythm. A two-minute phone call or email celebrating something positive can completely shift how a family sees you. Rather than the recipient feeling a sense of dread, you can make sure that the first thing that the parent/carer hears is positive. For example, you could use one of these openings for a positive call or email:

- 'I just wanted to let you know how proud I was of [child's name] today – they showed real resilience in maths.'
- 'It was such a joy to see [child's name] working so kindly with a partner this afternoon.'
- 'I thought you'd like to hear how confidently [child's name] contributed in class today.'

Early in my career, I once rang the same parent three times in two weeks, each time with a fresh tale of woe about their son's behaviour. By the third call, the parent sighed and said, 'Do you ever notice when he does something right?' Fair point. It was a turning point for me; since then, I've always made sure praise calls go out before I ever need to make a tricky one.

There are other times when you need to make sure that parents/carers know about things that haven't gone so well. These may be about behaviour or progress. The way you frame those conversations matters enormously. Some useful openers include:

- 'I wanted to speak with you so we can support [child's name] together.'
- 'I noticed [child's name] struggled with X today – have you seen anything similar at home?"
- 'This isn't about punishment; it's about helping [child's name] get back on track.'

Always pair the concern with a strength: 'Although today was difficult, I want you to know how well they did yesterday.' Families need to feel you see the whole child, not just the difficulty.

Parents' evening

Sometimes, it is possible to wait until parents' evening. This may be because the issue is not as pressing or because parents' evening is just round the corner.

No one really trains you for parents' evening, and it can feel like speed-dating but with higher stakes. Some conversation frames that you can lean on start with the opening lines:

- 'It's lovely to meet you—I've really enjoyed getting to know [child's name].'
- 'Before we look at data, let me share what I see in the classroom.'

Throughout, you should balance both the positives and challenges without ignoring the latter. The pattern is:

> Strength → area to work on → encouragement

In practice, this looks like: 'She can solve multiplication confidently. We're now pushing her to explain the reasoning behind her answers.'

As you end your parents' evening, these closing lines can be supportive and help end on a positive note:

- 'Thank you for coming in; your support really helps.'
- 'Here's our focus for the next half term – let's check in again soon.'

At my very first parents' evening, I was so nervous that I'd forgotten to bring half the assessment data. One parent asked, 'How is she getting on with chord progressions?' I blustered through a vague response. The parent paused, then said, 'So you don't actually know my daughter, do you?' Ouch. I learned quickly that knowing your pupils isn't just about warmth and relationships. It's also about preparation. Parents notice when you know their child well, and they notice when you don't. Turning up with genuine insight *and* the paperwork matters. Both are part of professional respect.

Stick to school policy. Follow your school's guidance on parent communication and partnership. If there isn't one, establish your own clear, professional boundaries from the outset and to keep it achievable. For example, 'I don't respond to emails after 6pm', 'I aim to reply within 48 hours', 'If I'm teaching and unavailable, please contact [office/staff member]'.

You should also introduce yourself early. A short flyer or email at the start of the year – 'All About Me' – is much better than trying to have a difficult conversation when they don't know your role or who you are within the school.

Finally, it is important not to take things personally. Families may be defensive or disengaged for reasons that have nothing to do with you.

Hannah Hall

Q How about when engagement from parents/carers is low?

A Sometimes families don't engage at all. They may have had years of difficult experiences with schools, where contact only came when something was wrong, or where they felt judged, dismissed, or blamed. Others may simply be carrying enormous life pressures: insecure work, health concerns, caring responsibilities, housing stress, or their own experiences of education that make school feel like an intimidating place. When families don't respond, it can be easy to interpret silence as disinterest. More often, it is about capacity, trust, or timing.

When engagement feels one-sided, the most important thing you can do is keep going. Continued, respectful attempts to make contact send a clear message: 'You matter, and so does your child.' Even when there is no immediate response, that consistency builds a foundation that may become important later. Varying your methods can also help. If emails go unanswered, a short phone call, a message sent home with the child, or a quick check-in at the school gate may feel more accessible. There is no single 'right' way to communicate; flexibility matters.

Approach families with curiosity rather than criticism. Instead of assuming reluctance or resistance, try language that opens conversation: 'I've noticed it's been tricky to get in touch – what's the best way for me to keep you updated?' This shifts the tone from confrontation to collaboration and signals that you are willing to adapt. You don't need to do this alone. Pastoral teams, SENDCos, family support workers, or colleagues who already have established relationships with the family may offer insight or support. Building on existing trust is often far more effective than starting from scratch.

One mindset that can be particularly helpful is *connect before you correct*. Before raising concerns or discussing what isn't working, invest time in building connection. Show families that you see their child's strengths, that you notice effort as well as difficulty, and that you value their perspective. When families feel respected and understood, they are far more open to difficult conversations. Correction without connection can feel punitive; correction grounded in relationship feels supportive.

Connection doesn't have to be time-consuming or elaborate. A brief message home sharing something positive, a quick phone call to celebrate progress, or a genuine comment about what a child enjoys or does well can make a significant difference. These moments shift the narrative so that contact from school isn't always associated with problems. Over time, this builds trust and reduces defensiveness on both sides.

Being proactive also matters. Don't wait for behaviour to escalate before making contact. A short introduction early in the year, explaining how you prefer to communicate and when families can expect updates, sets clear expectations and boundaries. Many teachers find it helpful to make praise calls or messages part of their weekly routine, rather than something that happens only when time allows. Consistency is reassuring for families and manageable for you.

It's equally important to protect your own wellbeing. Stick to your school's communication policies and boundaries. If these aren't clear, establish your own professional limits around response times and methods of contact. Not every message requires an immediate reply, and it's okay to be clear about when and how you are available. Try not to personalise family frustration. Anger, anxiety, or silence is rarely about you as an individual; it is usually rooted in fear, past experiences, or feeling overwhelmed.

Many teachers find it helpful to practise a few key scripts until they feel natural. Having language ready for difficult conversations reduces stress and helps you remain calm and professional. After each interaction, take a moment to reflect: What went well? What could I do differently next time? You will refine your approach quickly through experience.

Building relationships with families isn't an 'extra' you fit in once everything else is under control. It is part of the work of teaching. Strong home–school partnerships are among the most protective factors for children's learning, behaviour, and wellbeing. As an ECT, you won't always get this right – and that's okay. None of us do. But if you approach families with openness, consistency, and professionalism (and the occasional dose of humour), these relationships can become some of the most sustaining and rewarding parts of your career.

Hannah Hall

Q How can I work with parents and carers to understand and support the behaviour of pupils with SEND?

A Working with parents and carers is one of the best ways to support all pupils, and perhaps even more so for pupils with SEND. Families know their children best, and when schools build genuine partnerships, behaviour strategies become more effective, consistent, and compassionate. Yet I'm realistic, I know what it's like on the ground – collaboration isn't always straightforward. Time pressures, differing perspectives, and past experiences can all get in the way. The key is to actively listen to parents with empathy, openness, and a shared commitment to the child's wellbeing.

The starting point is always listening. Parents of children with SEND often feel (and sometimes are) unheard. They may have spent years explaining their child's needs to professionals, only to be met with scepticism, delays, and barriers. Beginning with listening shows respect but also helps you to understand. Asking parents what behaviours they see at home, what triggers they've noticed, and what strategies help can provide invaluable insights. Listening doesn't mean agreeing with everything, but it does mean valuing their expertise.

When discussing behaviour, it is important to share observations rather than judgements. It is easy to slip into language such as 'He's disruptive' or 'She refuses to work'. Instead, describe what you have noticed: 'He left the classroom during group work' or 'She put her head down when asked to read aloud'. This invites parents into problem solving rather than putting them on the defensive. It shows that you understand their behaviour may be a result of unmet needs in the classroom. It also models the kind of language we want children to hear about themselves.

Consistency between home and school is another crucial factor. Children with SEND often struggle with transitions and unpredictability. If home and school use very different approaches, behaviour can worsen. Working with parents to align strategies where possible makes a huge difference. If a child uses a visual timetable at home, replicate it in school. If parents use a calm corner, create one in the classroom. Consistency doesn't mean identical environments, but it does mean shared principles. And it means admitting and understanding that parents may be the ones to upskill us.

Respecting family context is vital. Every family has its own pressures, work commitments, siblings, financial challenges. Suggesting elaborate behaviour plans that parents can't realistically implement risks damaging trust. Instead, asking what feels manageable for them ensures that strategies are sustainable. Communication should be regular and positive. Parents often dread phone calls from school, fearing bad news. Regular positive communication changes that dynamic. Sharing successes, however small – 'He joined in group work today' or 'She remembered to bring her reading book' – builds confidence and makes parents more receptive when challenges arise. It also shows children that home and school celebrate their progress together.

Involving parents in planning is another way to strengthen collaboration. When creating behaviour support plans, inviting parents to contribute ensures that plans are realistic and personalised. Parents may suggest triggers you hadn't considered or strategies that work at home. Involving them helps parents have ownership, making them more likely to support the plan consistently.

Finally, acknowledging emotions is essential. Supporting a child with SEND can be difficult. Parents may feel guilt, frustration, or exhaustion. Acknowledging these emotions, without judgement, builds trust. Simple phrases like 'I can see how hard you're working' validate their experience and strengthen partnership. Importantly, working with parents and carers is never about handing over responsibility or expecting them to 'fix' behaviour. It's about recognising that we're all on the same team. And I believe that when schools and families collaborate, children feel supported, understood, and valued. Ultimately, behaviour becomes less about conflict and more about connection, which is what helps pupils with SEND flourish, not just in their learning, but in their confidence, relationships, and sense of belonging.

Georgina Durrant

Reflective questions

- What stories about behaviour might parents and carers already be holding about my school, and how might these shape how they see me and my classroom?
- How do my everyday actions and interactions (at the door, in emails, on the phone) contribute to the narrative of behaviour that families come to believe?
- When I talk to parents and carers about behaviour, do I focus on describing behaviour rather than defining the child, and how intentional is my language?
- How confident do I currently feel in having difficult conversations with parents and carers, and who can I draw on for support when I'm unsure?
- What is one small, proactive step I could take this term to strengthen relationships with parents and carers before problems arise?

Reference

Reay, D. (1998) *Class Work: Mothers' Involvement in their Children's Primary Schooling*. UCL Press.

7

A focus on safeguarding

Behaviour and safeguarding overlaps

Children's behaviour can often be a form of communication, expressing unmet needs, distress, or experiences that they may not yet have the words to articulate or even the cognition to really understand. Challenging or concerning behaviours can sometimes be an outward sign of risk, trauma, or instability in a child's life. As such, it is vital that all staff are equipped to look beyond the behaviour and with the lens of professional curiosity, asking ourselves, 'What is this child trying to tell us?'

However, safeguarding cannot only focus on those who push against boundaries or draw adult attention through disruption. Equally important are those children who remain quiet, the children who are too shy, anxious, or afraid to speak up. These children maybe internalising their distress, masking deep emotional needs or safeguarding concerns beneath compliant or withdrawn behaviour. The absence of noise is not an absence of need. Therefore, we have a responsibility to create a culture and be part of that culture where every child is seen, heard, and valued. A safe school environment is one where all

DOI: 10.4324/9781003592426-7

children – not just the loudest or most visible – are listened to, taken seriously, and given the opportunity to thrive. Safeguarding is not just about protection from harm; it is about proactively building trusting relationships and inclusive systems where children feel psychologically safe, emotionally supported, and confidently able to express themselves. In every interaction, policy, and behaviour response, we must hold in mind the quiet child, the scared child, and the unseen child, and ask ourselves what more we can do to help them feel safe enough to be fully themselves.

In this chapter, we explore the connection between behaviour and safeguarding, and why it is vital for Early Career Teachers (ECTs) to look beyond the surface of what children say or do. Some children express their distress through disruption, aggression, or refusal. Others internalise their trauma – hiding in plain sight through withdrawal, anxiety, or perfectionism. The absence of concern is not the absence of need.

That's why safeguarding must be everyone's business. It is not only the responsibility of the designated safeguarding lead (DSL); it's woven into every interaction, every policy, every lesson plan. This chapter encourages you to take a whole-child approach, recognising that behaviour is often shaped by circumstances we cannot see: instability at home, neglect, exposure to harm, unmet emotional needs. Safeguarding is not a form to fill in. It is a lens, a mindset, a relational act. It is about seeing the whole child – not just the behaviour they show, but the context behind it.

Whether you're responding to a disclosure, noticing something that doesn't feel right, or reflecting on a child's sudden change in mood, your role is critical. And while safeguarding can feel heavy at times, it is also one of the most profound acts of care and trust a teacher can offer.

Sara Alston and **Krupa Patel** explore how safeguarding and behaviour are deeply connected. Sara outlines how you can apply safeguarding principles within everyday classroom practice, while

Krupa emphasises that creating a positive environment is an integral part of safeguarding. Together, their work reinforces that behaviour cannot be separated from safety and care.

Q What is the role of school policies in safeguarding students, and how can I apply them as an ECT?

A Every school is different, but all of them must have the same basic policies that underlie their approach to safeguarding. These are structured by and supported by national guidance. The national guidance is divided into statutory guidance, which is legally binding, and non-statutory guidance, which is advisory. In England, the national guidance is published by the Department for Education. The core guidance that you need to be aware of includes:

- **Keeping Children Safe in Education:** This is the core statutory guidance for education settings. Everyone in every school must read and sign that they have read and understood Part one of this guidance. Staff should also read Annexe B which expands the information given in Part one. It is a good idea for staff to read Part five which is about sexual harassment and violence between children. The other parts are about the management of safeguarding (Part two), safer recruitment (Part three) and responding to allegations against adults (Part four). It is important to know that these exist as they may be important at some point in your career.
- **What to do if you're worried that a child is being abused:** This short piece of non-statutory guidance is a useful summary of the signs and indicators that a child might be experiencing abuse, neglect, or exploitation. Ofsted will check that staff have read and understood this document.
- **Working Together to Safeguard Children:** This major piece of statutory guidance is about how the different safeguarding partners – the local authority's children's services, police, and health should work together and alongside relevant agencies such as

schools, to safeguard children. It is a useful guide to the roles and responsibilities of these agencies as part of the safeguarding and child protection procedures. School staff need to know this guidance exists, but few who are not DSLs are expected to have read it in full.

- **Information Sharing: Advice for practitioners providing safeguarding services for children, young people, parents and carers:** This non-statutory guidance sits alongside *Working Together to Safeguard Children* and *Keeping Children Safe in Education*, and focuses on the rules and responsibilities related to information sharing.
- **Prevent Duty Guidance:** This statutory guidance applies to schools and organisations. It is part of the national counter-terrorism strategy. It provides the framework for the work in education to stop people from becoming terrorists or supporting terrorism.

These documents are further supported by guidance on a wide range of issues such as attendance, parental responsibility, and the use of phones in schools. The information from the core guidance is taken and used as basis for the school's policy. These may be written by the local authority or multiple academy trust, but they need to be personalised to reflect the needs of each school and their community. The core documents will include:

- Safeguarding/child protection policy which all staff must read. This is the 'what to do and why' document.
- Part one (and Annexe B) of *Keeping Children Safe in Education.*
- The staff code of conduct (sometimes called the staff behaviour policy). This is a vital document as it lays out the expectations of how the adults in the school should behave. By laying out what is and is not appropriate behaviour for the adults working with children, staff can be clear when adults are not meeting those expectations. Often this is unintentional and an error of judgement in the moment, so it can be challenged and corrected. Some 'push'

on these expectations will be from those who wish to make the unacceptable acceptable in schools as a way to abuse, harm, or exploit children. The code of conduct sets boundaries so that this is more difficult. Related to this will be...

- Whistleblowing policy. This document sets out how staff and others can and should raise concerns about adults' behaviour in school, including around safeguarding.

These documents will also include information on the safeguarding response to children absent from education and the role of the DSL and deputies.

All these policies apply to all staff regardless of the stage of their career or role. These are the procedures that underlie a school's ethos and approach to safeguarding. The procedures and ethos must be intrinsically linked. Both must be robust and followed to keep children safe. If you are not sure how any of them apply to you as an ECT, you must discuss this with the DSL and/or your mentor.

Sara Alston

Q How can I recognise and respond to safeguarding concerns in the classroom?

A It is vital that every member of school staff is familiar with and understands both their school's safeguarding policy and the most recent version of the statutory guidance *Keeping Children Safe in Education* (KCSIE). KCISE is published by the Department for Education (DfE) annually, and all school staff must read Part one and Annexe B to ensure that they fully understand what is meant by safeguarding and their responsibilities.

These pieces of guidance, alongside the DfE guidance, *What to do if you're worried a child is being abused*, are key reading to develop your understanding of what is a safeguarding concern. This should be further supported by training within your school. Everyone should receive safeguarding training as part of their induction. This should be updated at least annually. Staff are also supported by the school's DSL and their deputies. Any safeguarding concerns can and should be discussed with a member of your safeguarding team who can then help you record your concern following the protocols in your school.

Safeguarding and promoting children's welfare is defined in KCSIE as:

- providing help and support to meet the needs of children as soon as problems emerge
- protecting children from maltreatment, whether that is within or outside the home, including online
- preventing the impairment of children's mental and physical health or development
- ensuring that children grow up in circumstances consistent with the provision of safe and effective care
- taking action to enable all children to have the best outcomes.

Our safeguarding responsibilities apply to all the children in our care and are essential to keep children safe at home, at school and elsewhere in the community, on and offline. In addition to our general safeguarding duties is child protection work, which happens with a specific group of children identified 'as suffering or at risk of suffering significant harm'. This is regulated under Section 47 of 1989 Children Act.

KCSIE identifies that children's experience of abuse, neglect, and exploitation falls within four key areas:

- physical abuse
- emotional abuse
- neglect
- sexual abuse.

Teachers' concerns are rooted in the ways that children may communicate about their experience of abuse, neglect, and exploitation rather than working to identify the form of abuse they are experiencing.

Children will communicate their experiences of abuse in many different ways including through:

- what they say and how they interact with others
- how they behave (behaviour is communication – if you don't know and/or are unsure or even frightened to communicate something through words, you will do it through behaviour)
- their presentation
- their work and play.

Safeguarding concerns will include things that make you feel worried, uncomfortable, or bothered, and may include different things at different times. Occasionally, you may be faced with a disclosure where a child sets out to share a particular piece of information with you. In these situations, you must reassure the child, ensure that they are safe, and be clear that you cannot keep what they have shared a secret. You must not promise confidentiality, ask leading questions, speculate, or jump to conclusions. Listen carefully to what is said to you. It is not your responsibility to investigate the issue. Your job is to share the information with the DSL. Whether it is a concern or a disclosure, it is important that you share:

- the nature of your concern in as factual manner as possible
- what was happening and where the concern arose
- the exact words used by the child
- who else was present and/or involved
- the time and date
- if there is an injury. You need to record the details on a body map – ask your DSL for one.

With safeguarding, we need to be prepared to think the unthinkable. There will be children in our care who are experiencing abuse, online or offline, at the hands of family members and others in their community, strangers, other children, and even staff members. Whatever our concerns, we need to share them with the DSL immediately.

We need to remember that no single practitioner can have a full picture of a child's needs and circumstances. Everyone who comes into contact with the child has a role to play in identifying concerns, sharing information, and taking prompt action. We must not assume that others know or notice what we do. Something that seems minor may be a key piece of information to safeguard a child – you only have one piece of the jigsaw.

Sara Alston

Q What steps should I take to maintain a safe learning environment while managing student behaviour?

> Transforming the support and development offer for the teachers at the start of their career.
>
> Early Career Framework (Department for Education, 2019)

A This quote above demonstrates the role of support and development for ECTs. Even at the beginning of an ECT's career, their role includes maintain a safe learning environment for all of their learners. From this, context is essential. We must have a deep understanding of the communities in which we work, intersectionality, as well as our own biases that may shape our thinking. There are multiple lenses through which we can better understand how to maintain a safe learning environment:

- the practitioner's lens (personal and/vs professional)
- the learner lens
- family and wider community and their experiences.

For each, an ECT's own conditionings, beliefs, and experiences will shape how they show up, for themselves and others. This is an explicit reminder to delve into the culture of your setting and how ethos, vision, and values all align with practice to serve the wider community. In answering this question, I focus on how to maintain a safe learning environment and manage student behaviour while considering policy, professional relationships, active supervision, and the physical environment.

Clarity of policy, induction and expectations

As a new teacher, it is important to invest in understanding the setting's specific safeguarding policies as well as what these look like in practice. Every setting will have a DSL and a deputy for this role. If you are uncertain, then make sure you seek additional support to develop your understanding.

Luckily, the induction process will have a strong focus on safeguarding policy and practices. Use this time to clarify expectations and the systems for both practitioner and the learners. Safeguarding is everyone's business, and therefore being vigilant, listening, sharing all information, and using the systems are key. Having a clear and shared understanding of policies helps establish consistency and ensures everyone knows their roles and responsibilities. This clarity creates a foundation for accountability and trust.

As a new teacher, safeguarding can feel quite daunting; therefore, a few temperature tips may be useful:

- If something feels odd about a young person/group of learners, share it with the DSL.

- Make no promises; be clear you will need to share information with the DSL. Every member of staff in the organisation is part of the wider safeguarding team. You cannot keep information to yourself; therefore, report and record accurately.
- Make safeguarding a standing feature on your agenda with your mentor.

Impact of strong relationships

There are many competing priorities in education. You may be juggling planning and delivering effective lessons, and understanding data systems as well. You have to make sure that another priority is connection between you and your cohort of learners.

An underrated area for ECTs and even more experienced teachers is that of being relatable and approachable. Showing up authentically in a space where you are aiming to meet learners' needs is an area that is often underrated.

Part of this involves taking your time to get to know your students by learning their names, their current interests, and their strengths. Most importantly, aim to be consistent in your interactions.

A positive, trusting relationship inclusive of clear boundaries and clear reward and recalibration processes is critical for teachers to be emotionally available for their learners. A consistent trusting relationship is especially necessary for students with adverse experiences or additional needs as it provides them with a sense of security and belonging (Geddes, 2006).

Thinking points

Reflect on your own school experience.

- Which teacher made you feel safe and supported? Which teacher didn't?
- What were the key differences in how they interacted with you and others?

- List three qualities that helped you feel connected and valued:
    - ....
    - ....
    - ....

Use your senses and support staff for active supervision

Effective safeguarding requires knowing students, consistency of practice, and vigilance. Use all your senses to remain aware. Cues may include body language, change in personality (becoming louder or more withdrawn), change in attire and cleanliness. Even a change in a child's tone of voice may be an indication. Some may visually appear well, but they may have signs such as overuse of digital devices – and therefore ongoing dopamine hits, impacting their sleep and concentration – which can be an indication of potential risks.

Optimise your team in the room and collaborate closely with support staff, leveraging their expertise and insights to monitor changes and support with regulation.

Respond to behaviours with a trauma-informed approach

Understanding that behaviour is communication of an unmet need is crucial in fostering a safe learning environment. Often, it's rarely about the teacher; a young person may they feel safe enough to express their own true selves at that point in time.

Try where possible to de-personalise. Insist on quality mentoring and debriefs, and keep those effective reflection conversations open.

A trauma-informed approach encompasses responding with clarity, curiosity, and empathy, with a clear focus on underlying causes rather than just addressing surface behaviours. Therefore, carving breaks to reflect will enable you to build time for yourself to understand your responses to a given situation. This process is so insightful around developing your own self-awareness.

Restorative practice is a brilliant way to encourage self-reflection, allowing space to regulate and offering insight into deeper underlying causes (Hopkins, 2011).

Seek support from colleagues who can help you develop strategies to support yourself and the learners (Perry, 2006.)

Create a safe physical environment

The physical environment is often overlooked, yet it plays a crucial role in safeguarding and behaviour management, both in schools and alternative provisions. A clean, organised, and hazard-free space can help reduce anxiety and support de-escalation.

Features such as adequate lighting, good ventilation, and clearly marked areas contribute to a sense of safety and calm. Classroom layouts should allow for easy supervision and include quiet zones where learners can regulate if needed.

A thoughtfully designed and well-maintained environment – as highlighted by the *Broken Windows Theory* (Wilson and Kelling, 1982) – sends a strong message about care, safety, and expectations. Research shows that such environments positively influence engagement and behaviour, supporting a calm and purposeful learning culture.

Mentoring sessions to debrief and obtain support

To reduce the risk of overwhelm and burnout, treat your mentoring sessions as a safe space for reflection and open dialogue.

Use this time to seek guidance, discuss both challenges and opportunities, and listen to fresh perspectives. Shadow experienced colleagues and develop strategies to strengthen your classroom practice.

Mentoring and coaching are proven ways to support professional growth, retain staff, and develop effective teaching practice (Hobson & Malderez, 2013).

It's important that your mentor or coach is someone with whom you feel comfortable and able to show up authentically. If that isn't the case, don't hesitate to explore alternatives and advocate for the support you need to continue growing.

Conclusion

You matter, they matter, so keep talking about what matters, however hard the matter may be! This line has been one that enables us to keep our line of work aligned with purpose and accountability.

Maintaining a safe learning environment while managing student behaviour is a process which requires consistency, agility, and empathy. As an ECT, focus on clear policies and processes, and invest in relationships with your teams, learners, and families. Tuning in to what you see, hear, and feel in the room helps you understand what's driving behaviour and shape solutions that last.

Regular reflection and mentoring will embed and evolve safeguarding practices to meet the ever-changing needs of your learners.

Remember, safeguarding is about creating an environment where every learner can feel safe and belong, so they can thrive emotionally, socially, and therefore academically.

Krupa Patel

Reflective questions

- How can I build trust with students so they feel safe enough to ask for help?
- Am I paying attention to both the loud and the quiet signs a child might be in distress?
- What part do I play in making safeguarding a daily, lived practice, not just a policy?

References

Department for Education. (2019) *Early Career Framework*. Available at: https://assets.publishing.service.gov.uk/media/60795936d3bf7f400b462d74/Early-Career_Framework_April_2021.pdf

Department for Education. (2024) *Information Sharing: Advice for practitioners providing safeguarding services for children, young people, parents and carers*. Available at: https://assets.publishing.service.gov.uk/media/66320b06c084007696fca731/Info_sharing_advice_content_May_2024.pdf

Department for Education. (2025) *Keeping Children Safe in Education 2025: Statutory guidance for schools and colleges*. Available at: https://assets.publishing.service.gov.uk/media/68add931969253904d155860/Keeping_children_safe_in_education_from_1_September_2025.pdf

HM Government. (2015) *What to do if you're worried a child is being abused: Advice for practitioners*. Available at: https://assets.publishing.service.gov.uk/media/5a80597640f0b62302692fa1/What_to_do_if_you_re_worried_a_child_is_being_abused.pdf

HM Government. (2023) *Prevent Duty Guidance: Guidance for specified authorities in England and Wales*. Available at: https://assets.publishing.service.gov.uk/media/65e5a5bd3f69457ff1035fe2/14.258_HO_Prevent+Duty+Guidance_v5d_Final_Web_1_.pdf

Geddes, H. (2006) *Attachment in the Classroom: The Links between Children's Early Experience, Emotional Well-being and Performance in School*. Worth Publishing.

Hobson, A. J. and Malderez, A. (2013) 'Judgementoring and other threats to realizing the potential of school-based mentoring in teacher education.' *International Journal of Mentoring and Coaching in Education*, 2(2), pp. 89–108.

Hopkins, B. (2011) *The Restorative Classroom: Using Restorative Approaches to Foster Effective Learning*. Optimus Education.

Perry, B. D. (2006) 'Fear and learning: Trauma-related factors in the adult education process.' *New Directions for Adult and Continuing Education*, 2006(110), pp. 21–27.

UK Government. (2026) *Working Together to Safeguard Children: A guide to multi-agency working to help, protect and promote the welfare of children*. Available at: https://assets.publishing.service.gov.uk/media/69c2c4ce380a2a73a7cf9df4/Working_together_to_safeguard_children_2026.pdf

Wilson, J. Q. and Kelling, G. L. (1982) 'Broken windows: The police and neighborhood safety.' *The Atlantic Monthly*, 249(3), pp. 29–38.

8

Integrating perspectives

As we reach the final chapter of this book, it's worth pausing to reflect on what we've explored so far: the complexity of behaviour in schools, the emotional labour of being a teacher, the importance of understanding children as individuals, and the necessity of collective approaches across classrooms, schools, and communities.

This chapter is not about summarising each contribution – you've just read them – but about helping you to weave them together. It's about integration. Integration of knowledge, of perspectives, of strategies, and crucially, of *you* into the profession.

Behaviour isn't just about the children

A recurring feature of this book is that behaviour is rarely about the child. It's relational, contextual, and systemic. It is about communication, connection, and the culture of the school environment. Whether you're dealing with low-level disruption or navigating a safeguarding concern, your response sits within that wider system that you influence and develop by your actions.

DOI: 10.4324/9781003592426-8

It then follows that the answer to behavioural challenges will never come from a single strategy. No poster, policy, or consequence will work universally. Instead, what works is thinking systemically and relationally. It may start with you, but your work widens outwards.

The contributors to this book have shared sometimes conflicting approaches rooted in trauma-informed practice, structured systems, behaviourist theory, inclusive pedagogy, and more. This diversity is not a contradiction. It reflects what behaviour is – diverse, dynamic, and deeply human.

Thinking about practice

What this book offers is not just a toolkit (though it gives you many tools), but a mindset: a way of thinking and being in the classroom. The mindset is around curiosity and reflection.

Case study 1: The chaos classroom

Let's take a real-world scenario:

You've spent hours planning a lesson. It's engaging, incorporates adaptive teaching strategies, and is aligned to the school's curriculum. But within ten minutes of starting, one pupil is shouting out, another is refusing to work, and a third is rolling on the floor.

What do you do?

- **First, pause:** Regulate yourself before responding. As you read in Chapter 2, your own wellbeing matters. Your breath, tone, posture – all of these shape what happens next.
- **Use the strategies from Chapter 4:** Revisit your routines, calmly restate expectations, redirect attention.
- **Think back to Chapter 5:** What might this behaviour be communicating? Is the work too hard? Are they seeking connection?

- **Use your relationships (Chapter 4 and 5):** Draw on positive reinforcement for those getting started, and de-escalation strategies for those who aren't.
- **Reach out to colleagues (Chapter 3 and 6):** Reflect with your mentor, ask for another adult to observe or support, document and share what happened if needed.

Behaviour doesn't become easier because you gain magic powers with experience. It becomes easier because you become more attuned – to the classroom, the context, and yourself.

Case study 2: The 'difficult' parent

Another common challenge is working with parents and carers. Imagine this:

You've called home because a child has been repeatedly disruptive. The parent answers and immediately becomes defensive: 'You're always picking on my child. He says you don't like him. I'm sick of these calls.'

Here's how you might apply what you've learned:

- **From Chapter 4, 5 and 6:** Remind yourself that behaviour happens in relationship. Parents are often advocating in the best way they know how – even if that seems obstructive at times.
- Remember that consistency across staff (**Chapter 6**) is just as important when working with families, it can help build trust, reinforces messages, and protects vulnerable pupils from having mixed messages that might make it difficult for them to understand.
- **Stay calm and curious:** 'I hear that you're frustrated. I want to work together so your child feels safe and supported in school. Can we talk about what might help?'

- **Be clear about your observations, not your interpretations:** 'He refused the task and put his head down for most of the lesson. I'm wondering if he found it difficult or was feeling upset?'
- **Invite collaboration, not compliance:** "'What usually works well at home when he's feeling this way?'
- Log the conversation and seek support if needed.

Chapter 6 reminds us that teachers don't work in isolation. Parents, carers, mentors, and support staff are all part of the behaviour ecosystem.

Case Study 3: Behaviour or safeguarding, professional curiosity

A usually quiet pupil suddenly becomes aggressive in the playground. They push another child, scream at a staff member, and run away crying. Later, you overhear them muttering, 'You don't know what it's like at home.'

What do you do?

Refer back to Chapter 4 and Chapter 5. First, meet the behaviour with curiosity. What is this child trying to tell you?

Second, think safeguarding. As covered in Chapter 7, safeguarding isn't just about identifying harm; it's about noticing patterns and signals that something may be wrong. You are not being dramatic by raising a concern.

Document the incident factually. Share your observations with the designated safeguarding lead. Your role isn't to investigate, but to report what you saw and heard in line with the overall safeguarding policy. It's important to also remember yourself and whether you need support, as these critical moments can be emotionally complex.

Case Study 4: Being undermined by another teacher

You've been working hard to uphold consistent expectations in your classroom. But you find out that a colleague has told your class, 'Don't worry about that; I'm not as strict as Miss Patel.'

What do you do?

This is challenging, and many teachers will encounter it. Chapter 4 reminds us of the importance that consistency across adults is key to student behaviour. While it can feel personal, the best approach is professional.

If you feel safe to do so, have a respectful conversation. Try: 'I noticed the class were a bit unsettled after X. I think they're getting mixed messages about what the expectations are. Could we find a way to align more on that?'

You can also speak with your mentor to role-play the conversation or raise the concern more formally if needed. It's not about confrontation; it's about protecting the environment you're trying to create.

Case Study 5: I said the wrong thing

In a moment of stress, you say something you regret: 'Why are you always like this?'

Later, you see the student looking withdrawn and avoidant. You feel awful.

What do you do?

Start by owning it. As explored in Chapter 2, none of us are perfect. What matters is how we repair and go back. Go back to the child. Apologise. 'I was frustrated earlier and I said something I shouldn't have. That wasn't fair. I'm sorry. I care about you and want to support you better.'

Then move on and reflect. What made you respond in this way and, more importantly, what might you do differently next time?

Repair doesn't undermine your authority; it's an opportunity to model. It shows students that adults are human, but also responsible.

Although I have provided scripts and ideas, it is not about having the perfect script that you reel off. It's about building your own confidence to respond with integrity, empathy, and professionalism. As an ECT, you're unlikely to always get it completely right, but you also don't have to. What matters is how you respond and develop your practice. Keep returning and reflecting back on what you've learned.

Behaviour as care

Good behaviour policies and practices aren't about power; they should be about care. Caring what children are learning and how they feel safe and confident to learn as well as take manageable risks. Care doesn't mean letting things slide or avoiding crucial conversations. It means holding children to high expectations because we care. It means seeing their behaviour in the wider context.

As explored in Chapter 7, sometimes what presents as a behaviour concern may in fact be a safeguarding issue. Sara Alston's contributions on safeguarding show us that behaviour cannot be separated from child protection. A child who is withdrawn, angry, unpredictable, or explosive may be communicating something urgent. This is why understanding safeguarding is not a 'tick box'; it is an underpinning part of how we interpret behaviour.

As teachers, we are not therapists, but we do build relationships. We are not social workers, but we are key adults in children's lives.

We aren't perfect, but we are still a powerful presence for those that we support in school.

Building your own framework

This final section invites you to build your own behaviour framework. Not one lifted from a school policy, but one that grows with your values and practice. Consider:

- What do you believe about children's behaviour?
- What is your role in supporting it?
- What do you need to feel effective and emotionally safe in your classroom?
- Who are the trusted colleagues or mentors you can turn to?
- How do you keep learning?

Create a one-page reflective statement for yourself. It can include your guiding principles, strategies you've found effective, your boundaries, and your next steps. This isn't a formal document – it's for you.

Final thoughts

To the ECT reading this: you're not alone. You are entering a profession where people have thought deeply, cared passionately, and wrestled with these complexities for many years, and this book reflects that. The contributors have answered these questions in a way that reflects their own experiences and professionalism. I hope this will shape the way you might answer these very questions for new teachers in the future. Back in Chapter 1, we began with the honest confession many new teachers make: 'I'm here to teach, not deal with behaviour.' Hopefully, by now, I've made the argument that supporting behaviour is not separate from teaching. It's at the heart of it.

This book is not a panacea – you aren't going to feel one hundred per cent confident, and you are likely to still feel uncertain. That's okay. Uncertainty is not a weakness; it's how we shape our craft and develop professionally.

As you continue your journey to becoming the teacher you want to be, may this book sit dog-eared on your shelf, tea-stained and full of notes in the margin, ready to offer moments of reassurance when the days are tough. You are not just here to teach. You are here to build relationships, transform lives, and shape the future.

INDEX

Italic numbers indicate figures.

For Product Safety Concerns and Information please contact our EU representative GPSR@taylorandfrancis.com
Taylor & Francis Verlag GmbH, Kaufingerstraße 24, 80331 München, Germany

www.ingramcontent.com/pod-product-compliance
Lightning Source LLC
LaVergne TN
LVHW051201190826
845923LV00031B/433
* 9 7 8 1 0 3 2 9 7 1 5 0 6 *